Cross Fire

Cross Fire

by
Ole Anthony

Logos International
Plainfield, New Jersey

CONTENTS

15609

Acknowledgments

Special thanks go to my secretary, Mrs. Jean Watts, who has continued working when there was no money and apparently no hope; to Ruthanne Garlock who transcribed and edited the live interviews that were the source material for this book and to Orval, Mildred and Travis Frye who have been faithful in their constant prayers for this work.

Many times, if for some reason I was unable to be at the radio station, others hosted the program. Special thanks and recognition for this to Roy Cage, Jim Borom, Mike Burk and Glenn Jackson. Our gratitude is also expressed to the staff of radio station KDTX in Dallas, Texas, where *One Trinity Place* originated each night.

A thank you to each of the guests who appeared in this book and to the others who appeared on the program for taking time to share the reality of their experience.

—Ole Anthony, President
Trinity Foundation, Inc.

INTRODUCTION

We are living in a period of dramatic social unrest. Many governments are weak and unsteady. The social and economic systems of the world are in chaos, and more people than ever before are spurning the traditional moral, ethical and religious values in a ceaseless search for meaning and peace of mind. This search, in spite of its contemporary form, is the same search for a meaning for life, for a foundation; the same search for truth and honesty, that is common to all people in all generations.

About three years ago a small group of people began meeting together in Dallas. Even though our backgrounds and interests were different, we had one common denominator, each had come to the knowledge of Truth in our lives, Truth that went beyond religion or philosophy, a Way that became the bedrock and cornerstone for all activities within our lives. We each were interested in the fundamental question of how to communicate this beautiful simple Truth to a dying world.

This interest in communication was the origin of a nightly radio program called *One Trinity Place*, which is the the source material for this book. The program was sponsored by an organization in Dallas, Texas, called Trinity Foundation, Inc. *One Trinity Place* aired nightly for approximately two years. Its purpose was to introduce people to this Truth—not principles about truth, or what truth can do for you, or how to solve social problems with truth, but to simply meet and know and taste and touch Truth and Life.

Live interviews with over five-hundred people were presented to the listening audience. The guests on *One Trinity Place* were people who had received this strange gift of Life and lived it, but yet at the same time were honest enough to admit a restlessness and a longing for the haunting call of what is yet to be.

The thrust of the program was a sincere and honest talk-show format. It was totally unrehearsed. Everything was shared—doubts and certainties, troubles and solutions, questions and answers, defeats and victories.

The guests varied in personality and background, but they had one common denominator, they were all living to live, not living to die. They crossed all racial, ethnic and denominational bounds. They each had come to recognize one of the strangest of all paradoxes of life, that in order to be totally free, they had to be totally bound to a Person.

You may find this book to be different from what you are accustomed to. It may be a departure from standard forms of literary style. But our hope is that you will see, feel, and experience Truth and Life on every page.

—Ole Anthony—

CORRIE TEN BOOM

When one first meets Corrie ten Boom he is overwhelmed with a sense of stability, of inner peace, and of love that truly passes all understanding. Corrie has been tested in the fire. She spent several months in a Nazi concentration camp for helping Jews. Now she is in her eighties, yet she is vibrant and alive and "living to live." Her best known book is *The Hiding Place*, which has been made into a movie starring Julie Harris. She speaks in a charming Dutch accent, and there is a great deal of wisdom in what she says. Perhaps the best way to summarize Corrie ten Boom is to say she is like everyone's favorite grandmother.

CHAPTER 1

CORRIE TEN BOOM

It is a very great miracle of God when you can praise the Lord in tribulations . . . it is not cheap. False praise is like mush.

ANTHONY: We're sitting here in the Washington Hilton Hotel looking over the city of Washington, D.C. I can see the Washington Monument in the background, the White House and the Watergate Hotel are over to our left. Then I see a mass of buildings and cars and smog. Frankly, it looks like a mess. Yet we're sitting in a room and feeling and knowing full well the presence of God in this room, for God, Christ, and the Holy Spirit are in us. And that's the hope of glory. We have a very special guest today, a lady many of you have heard about or whose books you've read. She doesn't know the Lord from the standpoint of intellect or philosophy; she knows the Lord because He is in her. She has *experienced* the life of Christ. That's what we are going to talk about with our guest, Corrie ten Boom, author of, among other books, *The Hiding Place*. Corrie, it is nice to have you on our program. I know you have much to tell us.

TEN BOOM: I am very glad to tell a little bit of what I have learned in the long life I have lived. I am eighty-one, so I am an old woman. Sometimes, young people ask me, "How long have you known the Lord Jesus?" I always like to speak to young people; we understand each other. I ask them, "How long have you known the Lord Jesus?" And

2

they tell me, "Three days," or, "I have known Him for two years."

Then I say, "May I tell you something? I have known the Lord Jesus already seventy-six years. When I was five years old I asked Jesus to come into my heart, and He came in. And He has never let me down since that time. I have gone through very many experiences, but I can tell you this: when you know Jesus, the worst can happen in your life, but the best remains. And the very best is yet to be."

ANTHONY: Corrie, most of us know that you and members of your family spent many months in a German prison camp during the Second World War, but why did the Nazis send you there?

TEN BOOM: They sent us to the concentration camp for helping the Jews. When the horrible persecutions began to happen in front of our eyes to God's chosen people, a strange prayer began to develop deep within my heart. I was saying, "Lord Jesus, I offer myself for Your people, in any way, any place, any time."

Then the Lord began to open to us ways of serving and hiding Jews in our house. For this we were put into the camps and were privileged to share in Christ's suffering, and the reality of the Living Christ who carried us through it all.

ANTHONY: Did you learn from the suffering?

TEN BOOM: My sister, Betsie, died in the camp. Her last words to me were, "We must tell people what we have learned here. We must tell them that there is no pit so deep that He is not deeper still. They will listen to us, Corrie, because we have been here."

God's love still stands when all else has fallen.

ANTHONY: Can you really say with Paul that you praise God for tribulations?

TEN BOOM: No . . . perhaps, yes. Sometimes I wish I had not so many tribulations, but I praise God for what I have learned in the tribulations.

ANTHONY: There is a whole ministry now where people are saying the secret of spiritual progress is the power of praise. If your daughter dies, praise the Lord; if you get cancer, praise the Lord. Is that your understanding of the Scriptures?

TEN BOOM: I hope you are not shocked when I say "No!"

ANTHONY: I am not shocked.

TEN BOOM: It is a very great miracle of God when you can praise the Lord in tribulation. That is not something which is cheap, but it is a great miracle. It is possible, yes. I am so glad that Paul, who often went through many experiences which were not easy, said, "For those who love God, all things work for the best." (See Romans 8:28.) When I think of "all things" I sometimes think not of the difficult things, but of the happy things. I'm so glad that the happy times in my life, and the happy experiences I also have now, work for the best. But we can leave the program, the whole happening, up to Him who loves us.

ANTHONY: He's like a shepherd for the sheep; the shepherd sees a lot farther ahead of us than we do.

TEN BOOM: Yes, that is so. I believe one day we will see why, but I don't think we must always try now to find out why we have to go through deep water. You mentioned some very difficult things that happen, such as a child dying. When we know Him, the living Lord Jesus who has said, "Lo, I am with you always, even unto the end of the world," then we will experience that when the worst happens in our lives, the best remains. I have experienced that, for I was in concentration camps surrounded by people who had been trained in cruelties. And not only I. My sister Betsie whom I loved and who was very frail was there, and she starved to death. I knew my father, who was eighty-four years old, was in prison, and many of my friends were in prison.

Sometimes I said to my sister, "It cannot be worse than today." But the next day it was worse. Only those who have been in a concentration camp know what that suffering is. But in that time I experienced a very great strength in knowing, "I am not one moment without my Lord Jesus. He is with me always." That was such a reality that nobody could take that away. Now, it was not always a feeling. I had the feeling sometimes—and other times I talked it over with Him and said, "Lord, I look at the stars and I know stars have a certain way to go. You, with your Father, are guiding all those stars. Have you forgotten Corrie ten Boom?" The Lord did not say, "You may not say such things; I will not talk anymore with you. You are a naughty girl." Oh, no, He did not say that. The Lord said, "Listen to me; I'll have a talk with you. I can understand you."

ANTHONY: "My grace is sufficient for thee?"

TEN BOOM: That is so, yes. And you know, I like to speak about the love of the Lord Jesus. I believe in God the Father. It was because of His love that He has sent His Son, Jesus, to die and to live for us. But it is as if I know the Lord Jesus a little bit better than I know the Father.

I had these depths of not feeling that God was with me, then after that the Lord always gave me an experience. I can tell you, I believe even if I do not feel anything. That is because I believe in the Bible. When you ask why, then I can tell you not an intellectual answer, but because the Bible tells me. Then Betsie would talk with me, and the talks with her were all so great, and we were always together, night and day.

ANTHONY: This was in the prison camp?

TEN BOOM: Yes, in prison camp in Ravensbruck, in north Germany. We had to go to roll call at 4:30 in the morning. It was a terrible cruelty. We had to stand there for two hours. But the head of our barracks was so cruel, he sent us often a whole hour too early. Then from 3:30 we had to wait. But Betsie and I did not go immediately to the place where we had to stand for roll call; we made a walk over the whole camp. Everything was dark. There was no light, and everybody slept in the barracks. But then we walked with the Lord and talked with the Lord. Betsie would say something, I would say something, then the Lord would say something. How, I don't know. I can't describe it, but both Betsie and I understood it, and it was a little bit of heaven in the midst of hell. It was a reality.

When you are in very dangerous and deep and terrible experiences, then theology or theory or philosophy do not help you. Only a reality helps you. And I am so glad I have experienced the reality of knowing when you belong to Jesus, the worst can happen, but the best remains.

ANTHONY: And nothing can separate you from the love of God.

TEN BOOM: That is true. And that love of God I have never so experienced as I did in that time when I was surrounded by hatred.

ANTHONY: It is easy for us to make clichés of Scriptures. We don't always know what we are talking about; we just repeat it. It seems to me the Lord wants us to experience and to know the reality of the Scriptures.

TEN BOOM: It is true that when you go through the reality of deep suffering, you come into contact with the reality of God's answer. For when all the securities and answers of the world fall away, then you will understand what it means to have a living Savior. What a friend we have in Jesus! And He never, never, lets you down.

ANTHONY: But you have to be honest with Him, don't you? You can't hustle God, can you?

TEN BOOM: Of course not. You know, we have not to fight with flesh and blood, but with the very prince of the headquarters of evil. And the devil is like a good cow merchant who goes once around a cow and knows every weak spot.

ANTHONY: And then he whacks you.

TEN BOOM: Yes, and when there is something of dishonesty the devil sees that. It is true that this is one of the strongest tools in the hands of the devil, this dishonesty. We have to be honest. But you know, we cannot fool ourselves and others when we are in the ditch-depths of suffering. Then we have to be honest, for the suffering is honest. And then we have the reality. There is a Scripture which implies that false praise is like . . . how do you say in English? . . . mush.

ANTHONY: It seems that in Christ, after we have experienced and known Jesus, then we can praise God for we know He will take us through the suffering.

TEN BOOM: And He does exactly that.

ANTHONY: Do many people call you Corrie?

TEN BOOM: Many, many people call me Corrie. And children, they call me Aunt Corrie or Tante Corrie. I love children, and they love me. I like to talk to them, and they understand me.

ANTHONY: You get some fantastic answers when you ask children questions like, "Who is God?" or "Who is Jesus?" Really unbelievable truths that sort of slay our religiosity.

TEN BOOM: But Ole, you remember that Jesus said we must be like children to understand Him. I can tell you that God often reveals Himself more to children than to adults.

ANTHONY: Can you remember when you first met the Lord?

TEN BOOM: No. I was five years old, but my mother told me about it later. I remember that I was immediately an intercessor. I prayed for the whole street. Behind us was a street where there were many pubs, and I saw always drunken people. Mother told me later that every prayer ended with, "And Lord, will You save all the people in the Smeedestraat?" Now we smile when we think of a little girl five years old who prays for a whole street, but do you know that I have had answers to that prayer just one year ago? I spoke on TV in Ireland and a lady wrote me, "My husband was so interested that you have lived in Holland. He has been very close to you, for he lived in the Smeedestraat. And he knows now the Lord Jesus as his Savior." There I saw an answer to a prayer of seventy-six years ago!

ANTHONY: Isn't there something in the Bible that says, "And God was grieved because there was no intercessor?" Where is that?

TEN BOOM: It is in Ezekiel 22:30: "And I searched for a man among them who should build up the wall and stand in the gap before Me for the land, that I should not destroy it; but I found no one." God wondered because there was no intercessor. And that shows me that intercession is so important. I have read in the book of Revelation that our prayers are preserved. "And another angel came and stood at the altar holding a golden censer; and much incense was given to him, that he might add it to the prayers of all the saints upon the golden altar which was before the throne. And the smoke of the incense, with the prayers of the saints, went up before God out of the angel's hand" (Revelation 8:3, 4). That is so beautiful! Because that means there is not one prayer lost, for we are the saints.

ANTHONY: We really don't understand intercession, or the responsibility of results of intercession. I am a new Christian, and almost immediately after coming to the Lord I discovered there were many, many people I didn't know about who were praying for me. It is a tremendously humbling experience in the first place, but more important, God honors that. How many of us have loved ones who do not know the Lord?

TEN BOOM: We pray for them, and then the accuser, the devil, says, "Stop praying for that son, or that husband, or that daughter, or that brother, because you have prayed now so long. And you see, God doesn't answer." But the devil is a liar. There is not one prayer that is lost. All these prayers are kept in heaven, and someday we will see it. Sometimes God's mills go slowly, but they mill very securely. Is that good English?

ANTHONY: Yes, that's good English.

TEN BOOM: Go on praying for that person, for not one of your prayers is lost. And I have experienced it. I will tell you something. There came an old man to me—I say, "old man. . ."

ANTHONY: That's relatively speaking.

TEN BOOM: Yes, he was younger than I! He said, "When I was six years old I was in school, and my teacher was Miss ten Boom. Are you that Miss ten Boom?"

I said, "No, that was my sister." My sister was a teacher, and she loved little children. She always asked to remain in the first grade while teaching school. But very often my sister, Nollie, came home and said, "Mom, Betsie, Corrie, come—let's pray for my kids." And then we together prayed for these kids in her class.

Now this man asked me, "How is your sister?" And I told him the story.

ANTHONY: She is the one who starved?

TEN BOOM: No, this is another sister. But she had already died some years ago. Then afterward I said, "May I ask you, what did you think of the talk I gave?"

He said, "What do you mean?"

I said, "Well, I told you that the Lord Jesus says we have to be born again. We must be born a child of God to enter into and understand the kingdom of God. What do you think of that?"

He said, "That is no problem for me. I go every Sunday

to the church."

I said, "That is good, but a mouse born in a biscuit tin is therefore not yet a biscuit! To go to a church is not enough. To learn to know Jesus Christ and to be born a child of God is to open your heart for the Lord Jesus. He knocks at the door of your heart, and if you hear His voice and open the door, He comes in. And that is a reality. When you say a real 'Yes' to Jesus, that is so important the angels rejoice. Did you ever do that?"

He said, "No." And then he suddenly saw it, and that man did it. I had the joy to show him how simple the way is of accepting the Lord Jesus as Savior. I told him, "Jesus has said, 'Come unto me, all ye (and that includes you) who labor and are heavy laden, and I'll not send you away!' Now, there are many people who are heavy laden. But all you have to do is come to Jesus, and He will not send you away." And that man did it.

Do you see that? Years ago, my sister and Mom and me prayed for her class—just children six years old. I forgot it. But after many years, the Lord used me, who had prayed for him, to bring that man to the Lord Jesus. Such a great happening that the angels rejoiced! Now do you see that a prayer is not lost, even when it takes time before God answers? That is such a joy, and the Lord thinks it is so necessary. The Lord loves it when we pray.

ANTHONY: Right now I believe someone is listening who doesn't know the Lord Jesus. What would you say to him, Corrie?

TEN BOOM: I say to such a person, I have the idea that you know something must happen in your life, for you are a sinner. Jesus died on the cross for the sins of the whole world, and that is also for you.

He has said in the Bible, and the Bible is true, "Come unto me, all . . . " And that is also you, so it is for you. When you do not quite understand how it works, then you must just think: When I come to you and knock at the door and you open the door, what do I do then? Of course, I come in, because I have knocked. And the Bible tells that Jesus knocks at the door of your heart. When you open the door simply by saying, "Yes, Lord Jesus, come in," what does He do then? He comes in. And that is the great beginning. Because when you say "Yes" to Jesus, then He comes into your heart and He does that miracle in you so you are born into the very family of God.

And then the great joy begins, but also there is the fight. For there is not only a Savior, Jesus Christ; there is also the enemy, the devil. And he will try to take it away and make you believe it was not true what you said. But the joy is that Jesus has overcome the enemy. And now you must learn to listen to the Lord Jesus and not to the enemy. How can you do that? That joy is from the Holy Spirit, who makes your ears open for the voice of the Lord, and closed to the voice of the enemy. The Lord Jesus has laid His hand on your life; He lives in your heart—you don't understand it, but that doesn't matter. This is not a matter of understanding, but of faith. He lives in your heart by the Holy Spirit. Now you start to hear and understand His voice. The Bible becomes a love letter from God for you, and all the promises of the Bible are yours. *All* the promises.

You say, "Oh well, I do not know the Bible." That is so, but it is like a checkbook. All the promises of the Bible are written in your name and signed by Jesus Christ. But now you must endorse the checks. In Romans 5:5 I read, "The love of God has been poured out within our hearts through the Holy Spirit who was given to us." I say, "Thank you, Lord." Is it love I need at this moment? Then I have, as it were, endorsed the check. So now you must learn the Bible, for it is a message from God, who loves you.

I don't dare tell you that it is now so very easy. I

remember a movie star who said, "When I served the devil he left me in peace, but the moment I received the Lord Jesus, the civil war started." But it doesn't matter, because you stand on victory ground. I don't know you, but I know Jesus, and I know that Jesus is victor. He is the one to whom you belong. You are never alone. I can tell you that when Jesus is with you, when the worst happens, the best remains.

You must learn now to tell everything to Him. Talk to Him; listen to Him. You will experience that although it is a battle, it is a victorious battle. Hallelujah!

ANTHONY: I feel that some people came to know the Lord just then. From this moment on, never look to others; never look to yourself; look only to Jesus.

TEN BOOM: May I say something? Look around and be distressed; look within and be depressed; *look at Jesus and be at rest.*

MAJOR IAN THOMAS

One has no trouble telling from Major Ian Thomas' appearance that he is British. He has the bearing of what he is—a retired British Army officer. From a distance he may seem to be cold and aloof, but after visiting with him for a few minutes one senses a warmth and understanding that only comes from many years of walking and talking with God. Major Thomas is brilliant and articulate; his way of expressing his faith is truly amazing. He makes you listen; you know he is speaking Truth. His books include: *The Saving Life of Christ, The Mystery of Godliness,* and *If I Perish, I Perish.* This interview took place on the day the U.S. Congress had proclaimed as "The National Day of Humiliation, Fasting and Prayer."

CHAPTER 2

MAJOR IAN THOMAS

I don't want my hand to blow my nose when I want to scratch my back.

ANTHONY: Before introducing our guest for tonight, I want to share something he wrote:

"One night that year, just before midnight, I got down on my knees before God and just wept in sheer despair. I said, 'Oh, God, I know I am saved. I love Jesus Christ, and I am perfectly convinced that I am converted. With all my heart I want to serve Thee. I have tried my uttermost and I am a hopeless failure.'"

Then he goes on to say, "That night, things happened." We're privileged to have with us the man who wrote those words, Major Ian Thomas of England, a noted author and British evangelist. Major Thomas, what happened during the period just before and after those words of utter despair?

THOMAS: I came to know Jesus Christ when I was a boy twelve years of age, in a Christian camp, and I'm eternally thankful for those who then told me that He died that my sins might be forgiven. Quite frankly, it was almost the first time I had ever been exposed to that fact. I'd been taken to the camp by a friend who had one year previously accepted Christ, and he wanted me also to come to know the Lord Jesus. I can't be thankful enough for their concern in introducing me to the fact that Jesus died that my sins might be forgiven. But one thing I am sorry about—they forgot to tell me the Christ who died for me rose again to live in me.

If you lead a boy to genuinely accept Christ but you forget to tell him that the Lord Jesus who died for him rose again to live in him, how is he going to live the Christian life? You can only program him, and say, "The Lord Jesus has done His thing 2,000 years ago. Now He's gone back to heaven; He's left you down on earth to demonstrate your love and gratitude by your doing your thing." And it doesn't work. It isn't lack of sincerity. I can honestly say that from that moment in a Christian camp, I never once doubted my conversion. But I was given the rules of the game, I was programmed, and all I could do, in ignorance of the fact that the Lord Jesus risen from the dead lived in me to share His life with me, was to mobilize my own resources and try to play by the book.

To that end, I was concerned about the lost. I offered at the age of fifteen to become a missionary; I was leading a Christian group, and had massive, hectic activity for the Lord. I went to London University at the age of seventeen to study medicine, because I felt this way I could most beneficially serve God in Africa. But by the age of nineteen I was played out, frustrated. It was then that I got on my knees and said, "Lord, I'm sorry. I love You; I'll never doubt that I am redeemed. But quite obviously, I don't have what it takes."

ANTHONY: Major Thomas, I'm certain there are many in the audience who are either at or near that point of desperation. They love the Lord with all their hearts, they know beyond a doubt that they're saved and filled with the Spirit, but what they're doing has ended in total failure. What would you say to them? What happened to you?

THOMAS: I told the Lord, "I can't do it. It would be

quite unfair for me to go to Africa. It would be unfair to the
folks I would be going to; it would be unfair to You, God,
because I would be such a pathetic failure; and it would
really, to be quite honest, be unfair to me. I love You; if
there is anybody who's got what it takes, I'll stand by them.
I'll put a dollar in the plate, and I'll be there to help them.
But count me out; I'm quitting." And it was then I could
almost hear Him sigh with relief. The moment I told the
Lord I was going to quit, He said, "Thank you, that's what
I've been waiting for for seven years. Because for seven
years you've been trying to live for Me with the utmost
dedication, a life that only I can live through you."

At that moment of truth, the Bible split wide open.
Verses I had known, memorized and preached from, suddenly made sense. For me to live *is* Christ. Not to work for
Christ; not to mobilize my resources for Christ; not to
preach for Christ; not even to be a missionary or an
evangelist for Christ. But in all its sublime, mystifying
simplicity, for me to live *is* Christ. He is my life. To be alive
is Christ and to stay alive is Christ. There are all kinds of
verses like that: "I am crucified with Christ" for example
(Galatians 2:20). And this ". . . nevertheless I live; yet not
I; Christ lives in me. And the life I now live in this body
. . . " It's the same old body that you might recognize as
once inhabited by me, but I live through faith.

Faith is something most folks don't understand. Faith
isn't demonstrated by what I do for Him. My faith is going
to be demonstrated by what, in response to my faith, in
faithfulness *He does for me*. It's wonderful to grasp that fact.
"I am crucified with Christ: nevertheless I live; yet not I,
but Christ liveth in me: and the life which I now live in the
flesh I live by the faith of the son of God." That means I live
by a simple disposition that allows Him to be actually who
He is, as God, living His life, sharing it with me, and
demonstrating it through me. That is fantastic.

ANTHONY: That's the whole message—"Christ in you, the hope of glory."

THOMAS: The way it affected me more than anything else was discovering that the Lord Jesus is actually alive—not just in heaven, but in me. I could start saying "Thank you" for that, for which, for seven years, I had been begging. I had asked Him for strength, asked Him for help, asked Him for guidance, asked Him for victory—then, suddenly I realized that if He is alive, and alive in me, He doesn't give me strength, He is my strength. He doesn't give me victory; the victory is already won and He is just waiting to celebrate it. He doesn't give me wisdom; He is my wisdom.

ANTHONY: And on down the list. He doesn't give health; He is health. *He is* . . .

THOMAS: And our faith says, "Thank You."

ANTHONY: He is faith, too.

THOMAS: Well, we learn from Him the principle that He so marvelously demonstrated for thirty-three years when, in utter dependence upon His Father, He never ever took any step, made any decision, engaged in any activity other than in a relaxed attitude of total dependence upon His Father, and in His heart an unshakable confidence that His Father as God, in Him as man, could never ever be less than big enough. And He said, "As my Father hath sent me, even so send I you . . . ." (John 20:21). That's the divine simplicity of the gospel. It's great!

ANTHONY: Let nothing deter us from the simplicity which is in Christ Jesus.

THOMAS: That's true. Well, that was forty years ago, and I can say that nothing has changed the principle. I've found this to be the principle that almost shouts at you from every page of the Bible. God is telling us: first, Christ died to redeem us; secondly, He rose again from the dead by His indwelling Holy Spirit to share His life with us, to communicate that life through us.

ANTHONY: Across the country today we have had a day of humiliation and fasting and prayer. Do you think the Lord is going to honor any of that?

THOMAS: He has promised to honor those who will honor Him. And to honor God begins with the recognition in our own hearts that we need Him. Because sin isn't, in the first instance, an act. Sin is an attitude. All those things which we call sins are simply the manifestations of a state of heart. When man fell into sin he simply believed the devil's lie that a man could actually be man successfully without God. He embarked upon the mad experiment of human self-sufficiency, and God permitted it, because He had made man a moral being and had given him this moral option. So that's what happened when man believed the devil's lie—that man can be adequate without God, that he was self-sufficient—on the basis of his self-sufficiency he developed an attitude of independence. Created to depend upon the Creator, he stepped out of dependence into independence, and the moment you can afford to be independent you can afford to be disobedient. That is why true conversion isn't in clipping off certain things that are catalogued as wrong, because I can be proud of the things I don't do, and it won't change my heart.

ANTHONY: Like someone saying, "Look at me; I'm humble."

THOMAS: That's right. It simply magnifies my own egotistical self-worship. True repentance is trading the attitude of independence for dependence, so that by a deliberate act of my choice I step back from my independence into dependence. And that's where true worship begins. That's where honoring God begins.

ANTHONY: But that is not just one time. You have to do it ten times a day, a hundred times a day, a thousand times a day.

THOMAS: It's what I call continuous repentance. This isn't morbid, and it isn't introspective. It's simply facing the facts of life—that God actually made man in such a way that God's presence in man is imperative to his humanity. If I admit that I need God for every step that I take, if I am prepared to admit my weakness every step that I take, that isn't morbid introspection. An oil lamp was created in such a way that it produces light only by virtue of the fact that there is oil in the lamp to sustain the light. Suppose I were to ask, "Why does an oil lamp need oil to produce light?" Without making the answer complicated it would be simply, "It was made that way." You can detach the lamp from oil and you've still got an oil lamp, but it won't behave like one. It is useless. There is no life in the lamp. What would be the remedy? To put oil back in the lamp.

Now, if you can imagine a lamp capable of thought, saying, "Without oil I can do nothing, I am nothing," isn't morbid introspection. It is simply a lamp facing the facts of life. "I was made that way. I was created to contain oil, which alone can sustain the light. So I was created to adopt an attitude of dependence upon that which I must receive in order to fulfill the function for which I was made."

ANTHONY: That's a recognition of dependence. When you try to share the life of Christ most people either say, "Of course I'm a Christian; I'm an American, aren't I?" Or they say something like, "I don't want to be a Christian because I have to give up too much." Or they say, "God helps those who help themselves." Is that same attitude prevalent all over the world?

THOMAS: Yes, I believe it is. It happens to be the nature of my ministry that I have to travel in many parts of the world. And folks are all the same, whether they're students, or apprentices, old men, or young. Basically, we're all the same beneath the surface, and every heart knows its own weakness. We're just too proud to admit it, and therefore we live in self-imposed poverty.

But God is merciful; God is full of compassion. God is waiting to fill our lives with incredible plentitude, if only we will admit our bankruptcy. That is why I believe that a call from the Senate and Congress of this nation is an encouraging sign. And God won't despise it. It certainly isn't adequate in itself; and there will no doubt be countless hundreds of thousands who will have gone to church and "tipped their cap" as it were to God, in the hope that things may get better. There may even be a selfish motivation. But even in the imperfection of the gesture, the very fact that a nation has paused to consider God is encouraging.

ANTHONY: This is the first time I have ever voluntarily fasted, and it has been a rather amazing experience for me. I had every intention not to do it. But the closer we got to this day, it was a certainty that I had to. All day I've been starving. But things have been revealed, just simple little things that I'd never thought of before. Habit patterns that I wasn't even aware of. These things about me have been revealed through this experience of fasting. Is that a common thing one undergoes?

THOMAS: I think it may well be. Perhaps it is not just the physical act of fasting, but the attitude of mind, you see.

ANTHONY: Because otherwise, fasting could be legalistic.

THOMAS: If you try to buy His blessing or His favor by the length of your fasting or praying, you might just as well have a prayer wheel, or some tin god. It is always the attitude that counts. Paul said, "Present your bodies a living sacrifice, holy, acceptable unto God, which is your reasonable service. And be not conformed to this world" (In other words, don't ape the world's way) "but be transformed by the renewing of your mind" (Romans 12:1, 2). The word "mind" there means attitude or disposition. The transformation of character takes place by a renewing of that attitude.

What is the renewed attitude that I'm to adopt? We're not left in doubt about that. In Philippians Paul says, "Let this mind (or attitude) be in you, which was also in Christ Jesus" (Philippians 2:5). What was His attitude? For thirty-three years, he displayed an attitude of total, unrelenting dependence upon His Father. If there were 5,000 to be fed miraculously, He bowed His head and said, "Thank You." Whom does He thank as He takes the five loaves and two fishes? He doesn't thank Himself. He thanked His Father and demonstrated the principle of human dependence.

When Lazarus was to be raised from the dead, Jesus looked up and said, "Father, I thank You that You have heard me." The explanation He gave in the 11th chapter of John was this: " . . . so that they may know You sent me." That's the mind which was in Christ Jesus.

ANTHONY: There are people in the audience who have had the same experience you've had. They have worked for maybe several years or a lifetime doing things *for* God. How do they come to that transformation of not doing things *for*, but depending on?

THOMAS: Well, they've got to recognize the purpose of God in redemption. When the Lord Jesus died upon the cross as a redemptive transaction, it was to allow a Holy God (without doing violence to His own righteousness, because sin now to His holy and eternal satisfaction had

been dealt with) to restore to man through the gift of the
Holy Spirit that life that was forfeited in Adam when he
repudiated the relationship of dependence on God that let
God be God in the man. So the purpose of His death for us
was literally that He might put His life in us.

Why does the Lord Jesus die for me so that His life by
the gift of the Holy Spirit can come back into me? Because
without Him I can do nothing. If I learn from that, it means
that from now on, for every step I take, every situation into
which that step takes me of threat or promise or opportunity
or responsibility, it will become increasingly a disposition.
It won't happen all at once. I've got to practice the principle
until it becomes a disposition. In every situation I must bow
myself out, bow Him in, and say, "Lord Jesus, thank You.
You not only died for me, You rose again to live in me, and
as God living where You do in my heart, I know that You're
big enough for this situation, and I'm going to thank You.
You'll need hands; here they are. You'll need feet; here they
are. You'll need lips to speak with; I'm at the receiving end
of Your instructions."

In other words, we must not get the idea that this is
passivity. We don't go around with a glazed look in our
eyes and our mouths open. It's our bodies He is going to
use, our hands He's going to work with, our lips He's
going to speak with, our minds He's going to think with.
But the fantastic thing is, He actually, experientially, in-
dwells us and will by the Holy Spirit function within man's
soul and motivate our activity. I'm going to feel that. I don't
have to try to work it up as a sort of emotion. I have an
unshakable confidence that He, as God, being Who He is
and living where He does, in me, has what it takes to
motivate me into action in such a way that my flesh and
blood will actually clothe His mind and will and purpose,
and give it a valid expression of what He is about.

That is what it means to be a member of His body. That's what I expect of the members of my body. I don't expect them to demonstrate their own enthusiasm on my behalf; I expect them to be in an attitude of restful availability and instant obedience the moment I want them to do something.

ANTHONY: You don't want your thumb to go around praising you?

THOMAS: I don't want my hand to blow my nose when I want to scratch my back!

ANTHONY: It seems to me that our lives should be praise. Am I wrong there?

THOMAS: No, you're absolutely right. Again, it gets back to disposition. We tend to be too experiential. We always want to feel something.

ANTHONY: Oh, we can feel something if He wants to let us feel it.

THOMAS: Of course, that's perfectly true. But supposing the expression of His joy in me at this particular time is that sensation or this. I've got to avoid the danger of supposing that *without* that sensation or this, I haven't got true joy. We tend to depend on our feelings. This has always been true. There may be a true, genuine manifestation of the Spirit of God's power in a certain location for a particular situation that is absolutely valid. The mistake we make is to take photographs of it, try to reduce it to a formula, analyze it, publish it as a little book, and then reproduce it. Then we feel that must be the format, and unless that format is reproduced somewhere, then we haven't got a true manifestation of the Spirit of God.

ANTHONY: One of our guests one night said, "If you're giving yesterday's testimony, you're not in the will of God." How would you respond to that?

THOMAS: That's perfectly true. The Lord Jesus doesn't live yesterday, He lives today. I remember a lady called me while I was in Chattanooga and said, "I know exactly what you're talking about; five years ago I had that experience." And I believe she may well have enjoyed the life of Christ at that time in appropriating His presence in her heart. But she said, "I lost that experience, and for five years I've been asking God to give it back to me." And of course that was her mistake. I said, "Lady, He will not give you that experience back, because the Lord Jesus isn't living five years ago; He's living today. You don't want that experience back. You want to get back to where you belong, in your spiritual union with the One who is as alive in you now as He was then. Let Him be Himself, manifesting Himself through you. Share His life."

ANTHONY: That is a beautiful way of putting it.

THOMAS: Think how many people worry themselves silly about the will of God, because they imagine that the will of God for their lives is something future. "One day, God will reveal to me His will." But the will of God isn't anything future. The will of God for your life and for me is Jesus Christ. If I am a member of His Body in healthy spiritual union with the One Who, having died to redeem me, rose again from the dead to indwell me, and if it's really true to say, "For me to live is Christ," then what is the will of God for me tomorrow?

ANTHONY: Jesus Christ.

THOMAS: Jesus Christ, being allowed by me, as a member of His body, to be Who He is as God, clothing His divine activity with my humanity. It's hilarious! And what's the will of God for my life day after tomorrow? Jesus Christ. Except that tomorrow won't be tomorrow when it comes; it will be today. And the day after tomorrow won't be the day after tomorrow anymore; it will be today. So how many days at a time do I live? Just one day at a time, restfully relying upon the fact that the Lord Jesus, as

God, living where He does in my heart, can never ever be less than adequate for every situation that's going to arise.

ANTHONY: Someone might be saying right now, "Well, that sounds good, but what about me? I've got to pay some bills tomorrow." Or, "I've got a family and I've got a husband who is always hollering at me, and I've got kids clamoring for attention. That's fine for him, but what about me?"

THOMAS: Well, we've got to learn the true significance of committal, which is to put it right down on the ground and take our hands off it. You see, what we normally do when we say we commit a situation to God, is to bring it to Him and say, "God, doesn't that stink?" Having let Him have a sniff, we then carry it away and we think that's committal. That isn't committal. It is to put the situation right down at His feet, take our hands right off it, and then withdraw and say, "God, I don't know how You're going to handle it. Humanly speaking there doesn't seem to be any possible solution. But I'm going to thank You for Your adequacy. I have no preconceived notions as to what You are going to do or when, but I'm going to rest in Your incredible fidelity. Thank You, Lord."

ANTHONY: Major Thomas, are you telling me that that really works?

THOMAS: I believe with all my heart it works. From the moment when in sheer despair I said, "Lord Jesus, for the first time in seven years since I first received You as my Redeemer, I'm going to dare to thank You, in advance of any evidence, with nothing but a history of failure . . . . " From that moment God vindicated His utter integrity, and nothing has changed the principle in forty years.

ANTHONY: Why do so many ministers and evangelists seem to have problems with and about money?

THOMAS: So often, money has been made a criterion of God's seal of blessing. In other words, if money is available, that means God is in it. Nothing could be farther from the truth. The fact that you can raise money to promote a certain objective doesn't necessarily mean it is in the plan of God. It simply means you're good at raising money! Some people are good at it and some are not. But if that is the ultimate criterion then there are lots of way-out organizations that must be much in favor of God, because they certainly know how to rake it in. But that isn't it at all.

Money is never the ultimate criterion of God's favor or God's blessing. There's only one thing I have to know in any given situation: not whether it is possible; that is to say, whether the support is available, whether I've got the personnel needed. It isn't a question of "Is it possible?" There is only one issue you and I have to face in any situation: "Is it right?" There are lots of things we can make possible that will never be right in God's purpose and plan. But there are countless things that are right which, humanly speaking at this moment, are utterly impossible. But He is the God of the impossible.

So let me have an open heart and trust Him with all my heart. That means I must yield to Him my mind, my emotion and my will. It is important that we understand the expressions we use. We learn evangelical jargon that often has little substance in our understanding. We don't take the lid off and look inside to see what the content is. What is it to trust God with your heart? What is your heart? It is your mind, your emotions and your will. And to trust God with your heart means that you're going to let Him function within your soul. If somebody says to you, "My car is in the garage for repair. I urgently need transportation; would you mind if I borrow yours?" you would say, "Of course not, go ahead." You are confident the man is trustworthy, and he is a competent driver. Now, having trusted him with your car, what do you expect him to do with it? Drive the thing!

When you trust God with your heart, what do you expect Him to do with it? Think through your thinking, react through your reactions, decide through your deciding, actually *be God* by His Holy Spirit, functionally in business.

The Bible says, "Trust in the Lord with all thine heart; and lean not unto thine own understanding. In all thy ways acknowledge him . . . "(Proverbs 3:5,6). Give Him the absolute right as God to be God in action. And what does He promise to do? Govern your behavior. That's what He means. "I will direct your paths. I will govern your behavior in any given situation, in response to your attitude, disposition of utter trust, in a way of which you will be totally unaware and unconscious. Even though you pursue the normal processes of thought, you will draw conclusions in a way you'll never be able to understand or explain. By My Holy Spirit I'll be thinking through your thinking, reacting through your reacting, and deciding through your deciding."

So make your decision. When the phone call comes and you have to give an answer, make the decision. Don't consider yourself infallible, but don't have a post-mortem.

ANTHONY: The apostle Paul said, "We have this treasure in earthen vessels . . . we are troubled on every side, yet not distressed; we are perplexed, but not in despair . . . " (2 Corinthians 4:7, 8). It's not always what the flesh may like, is it?

THOMAS: No, God never promises that we will be delivered from threats and dangers. But we can have utter peace in the middle of it all, in the unshakable confidence that Somebody is in business who is gloriously competent. Well, that's marvelous to have that inner conviction. You can't have victories unless there is a battle. But the marvelous thing is that the issue is already settled in heaven, because we have the life of the Victor!

ANTHONY: What does sonship mean to you, Major Thomas?

THOMAS: In terms of my relationship to God?

ANTHONY: Yes.

THOMAS: The restoration to me of that life that I was created to share by the restoration to me of the Holy Spirit, through whose presence I actually at this moment share the life of Christ and live together with Him. And He, in His indwelling presence, bears witness with my spirit that I am God's child. The birthright of God's children now redeemed in the blood of His dear Son and indwelt by His Spirit, is to share His life. That is sonship to me.

ANTHONY: A joint-heir with Christ—that's heavy.

THOMAS: The illimitable resources of deity are constantly available to me, not because He gives me something, but because of Who He is, living where He does.

ANTHONY: If the world could only know who Jesus is! Not our doctrines, just who He is. If we lift up Jesus, He will draw all men unto Himself, right?

THOMAS: Of course, and this is where we have to avoid the danger of cherishing the gifts more than we do the Giver, idolizing the blessing rather than the Blesser.

ANTHONY: I looked at Jesus and the dove of peace flew into my heart; I looked at the dove and he flew away.

Major Thomas has written several books: two of them are, *The Mystery of Godliness*, and *If I Perish, I Perish*, published by Zondervan Publishing Company. Do you like to write?

THOMAS: I can't say that it excites me. I wish I had the time to write more. But it's the time that is a problem.

ANTHONY: It takes a lot of discipline to write. Does it take discipline to yield?

THOMAS: I believe it does, yes. We're not to be flabby in our Christian lives, we're to be soldiers. In other words, we've got to learn obedience. Faith is obedience. In the Chinese language there is only one word for obedience and faith, because they equate the one with the other. So although I've got to avoid the rigidity of pure legalism, God never compels me, so that my compliance to His demand will always be in the response of obedience.

ANTHONY: He never violates your will, does He?

THOMAS: He never once violates my options. And therefore obedience is the only valid expression I can give of my dependence on Him.

ANTHONY: You say you've been in Christ for forty-seven years. Have you found that when it comes time for those decision points in your life—and I'm sure you can go back and categorize several major decisions in your life—has there sometimes seemed to be an easier way out of the difficulties and situations?

THOMAS: Yes, there has been. I believe Satan will always give you the reasonable alternative to faith, because so often the obedience of faith involves a margin of difference between what is considered to be humanly possible, and what is actually only divinely logical. Divinely logical because there is a hidden factor—God Himself—that would be absent in human reason.

This is what Abraham had to face between Ishmael and Isaac. What was the reasonably possible? Ishmael. Bring Hagar, the bondwoman, because his wife was barren and had never borne children, and now she was beyond the age of bearing. So the reasonable alternative to faith was Ishmael. And of course Abraham had to take care of that baby, and it kicked, and still kicks. Now supposing he had adopted the right disposition from the start when God said he was going to have a son, which humanly

speaking, was impossible. His disposition of faith would
have been to say, "God, You say I'm going to have a son.
Humanly speaking, that is a sheer impossibility. But that
isn't my problem, because I didn't tell You; You told me. So
thanks very much. I haven't a clue how You can do it, but
I'm available."

A year later he would have said, "God, a year ago You
told me I was going to have a son. It was impossible then,
but I'll tell You something. It's one year less possible now."
And in ten years' time he would have said exactly the same
thing. But fourteen years from the time the promise had
been made, Isaac would have been born, but there would
have been no Ishmael. And the world would have been
saved quite a lot of problems.

If only we would learn the sheer simplicity that lets
God do the impossible. It isn't recklessness. He doesn't ask
us to be reckless. We've got to maintain that attitude toward Him that allows Him by the Holy Spirit to build up in
us a solid conviction that this step, this decision, this action
is right.

ANTHONY: You've got to keep the oil in the lamp.

THOMAS: That's right.

ANTHONY: A listener just called and said she was
born again while reading the first page of your first book,
The Saving Life of Christ. It must be powerful if she was
born again reading the first page!

THOMAS: Well, it doesn't surprise me a bit, because
the Holy Spirit delights to honor the Lord Jesus. If there is
an awakened soul, the Holy Spirit can exalt the Lord Jesus
and He becomes real in the experience of the one who then
mixes that word of truth with faith. It's wonderful.

ANTHONY: Besides your salvation, what has been
the most meaningful experience that has happened to you?

THOMAS: It is difficult to select one, but I would say
the greatest gift God has given to me in my Christian minis-

try is a very sweet and lovely Christian wife whom I believe
God chose. I thanked God for her for six or seven years
before I met her, knowing He must give her to me as He
must give me to her, if our lives were to be genuinely
identified in His purpose and plan. And if ever I suppose a
man needed the kind of wife that God had to give him, I've
been that kind of man—home only for two weeks since last
August, and never a complaint. Only the sweetest encouragement. I did have the privilege of her company in Aus-
tralia and New Zealand for a couple of months, but then I'll
be away for four or five months again without seeing her.
But the only thing she'll write is, "When there is no blessing, come home." And that is a wonderful gift from God.

ANTHONY: One of the things most misunderstood in
my life is the importance of the local church to me.

THOMAS: Of course there is only one church that God
recognizes, and that is the fellowship of redeemed sinners,
the Body of Christ that knows absolutely no artificial bar-
riers as between man and man or race or creed or class or
color. The only valid church is the one maintained in
heaven. It is matched on earth by those on earth who are
still alive and in the Body by the presence of God the Holy
Spirit within the human spirit of every forgiven sinner. So
there will be no mistakes. Nobody will get in who
shouldn't be there; nobody will be left out who should be
there. For the names are written in the Lamb's Book of Life,
and that is sealed by the presence of Christ Himself
through the Holy Spirit within the redeemed humanity of
that individual. Now that is true of the whole wide world.

But at the same time, I believe emphatically that God
has so ordained that of that worldwide church there should
be a local expression in the assembly or the fellowship of
believers. And I believe it is imperative to the spiritual
well-being, not only for the individual, but for the Body

itself, that we should not forsake the gathering of ourselves together. In other words, although I believe an immense amount of profit is being derived from little home Bible study groups, this should never be a substitute for that solid expression of the local church. I couldn't care less what it calls itself, so long as it is solidly established upon the authority of God's Word, derives its life from the person of Jesus Christ exalted as Lord in the heart of each individual, and worships corporately by those who recognize themselves to be members individually and in particular of His Body corporate. So the local church is to be the Book of Acts, to go out into the community and to penetrate to the uttermost ends of the earth.

TOM LANDRY

To the world's eyes, Tom Landry, head coach of the Dallas Cowboys, is a celebrity. He was a champion both as a player and coach. As a player, his team, the New York Giants, won the national championship in 1956; as a coach, his team, the Dallas Cowboys, won the Superbowl in 1971. In the press he is called the "ice man" because of his unemotional public stance. But in person he is warm, humble and honest. He has had a great impact on many thousands of lives. His faith has given him the ability to bounce back after humiliating defeats. One cannot help liking Tom upon meeting him, and I am sure you will like him after reading this chapter.

CHAPTER 3

TOM LANDRY

After achieving everything I wanted the emptiness was still there.

ANTHONY: There is a Scripture in the Beatitudes that says, "Blessed are the poor in spirit: for theirs is the Kingdom of heaven. Blessed are they that mourn: for they shall be comforted" (Matthew 5:3, 4). But then comes one that is a real problem. It says, "Blessed are the meek: for they shall inherit the earth" (verse 5). Somehow, in my mind, I cannot imagine a man like Tom Landry (who is our guest tonight) as meek. What does "meek" mean to you, Tom?

LANDRY: When you think of somebody meek you usually think of somebody who is rather passive. But I'm sure Christ did not mean it in this way. I haven't really researched it, but I know He didn't intend for meekness to mean passivity. He was such a strong person Himself, that He couldn't have meant it in that way. It has to have a deeper meaning than that.

ANTHONY: One explanation of meekness I've heard is that meekness is a Clydesdale horse—one of those huge 2,000-pound horses—with a harness on, and Christ in the saddle. I think that is a more apt picture of meekness than the mistaken picture we tend to have.

LANDRY: Yes, I'd like to have about eleven of those working for me! I don't think "meek" means weak at all.

ANTHONY: Let's talk about Christ in Tom Landry.

You have been a Christian since 1958. Can you tell us something about what led up to your conversion?

LANDRY: I was a churchgoer from the time I can remember. My dad was superintendent of a Sunday school in the small town where I grew up, and I didn't have much choice. I was in Sunday school every Sunday because he was the superintendent. But it really didn't mean much to me.

As an athlete, and even as a youngster, I thought in order to be happy and to have an abundant life, you had to be successful in whatever area you went into. Football was everything to me; it was my religion. So I kept setting goals and achieving, setting goals and achieving, but each time I achieved a goal, I felt restless and empty. I always wanted to do something else. I wanted to reach that goal in life where I would have happiness and everything that goes with it. Though I had great success in athletics and in professional football, I never did achieve it. I always kept rationalizing, as many people do who seek for success in a material way, that I had an ideal out there, and if I could just reach that, everything would be okay. To me, as a player and a coach, I had to be the top player or have the top team in football.

It just so happened in 1956 when I was with the New York Giants, we won the world championship. We beat the Chicago Bears 47-6 in Yankee Stadium, and you can imagine the thrill we had after seeking a goal like that for so long. And I was the most surprised person in the world when that emptiness came back. I thought it was gone, because I had never experienced anything like winning that championship.

Basically, I was really mixed up. In my profession I had gone all the way through, I had accomplished all the goals I had set, I had reached the top. And yet it wasn't satisfying to me. I was ready to stop coaching and go into business. I was preparing myself for the business world, because I thought that was the place I would find it.

Then one day I ran into a friend of mine on the street here in Dallas who said, "Tom, how about attending a Bible discussion group with me at the Melrose Hotel?" You can imagine what I thought. I had been to church every Sunday for as long as I could remember. I knew the Christmas story, I knew the Easter story, and I thought, "What do I want to study the Bible for?" But he was a good friend and I went with him.

We got into the Gospel of Matthew and the Sermon on the Mount. We talked about the Beatitudes. It really changed my life completely, because I heard the gospel of Jesus Christ for the first time. I didn't even know what the gospel was. I'd heard it all my life; the ministers I'd heard had challenged me. But I didn't have ears to hear, and I hadn't comprehended it. Then all of a sudden it became clear to me. I did not reach the point of saying, "Today I understand it so much that I accept Christ and invite Him into my heart." It was a gradual thing, but all of a sudden I knew Christ was there. And then I committed myself to Him.

My priorities changed: God became first. But my ambitions did not change. I still wanted to be the best football player, the best coach, and have the best team. But my perspective on everything changed. I realized I could not achieve happiness and the abundant life without putting Christ first. It was a great discovery, but it took me thirty-three years to find that out. I've told many youngsters and athletes that if I could change my life, I would pray that just one thing could have happened—that I would have committed my life to Christ when I was a youngster. I missed such a great enjoyment of all those accomplishments I made through the years, because each time I accomplished something there was an emptiness and a restlessness about me.

ANTHONY: Did the church you attended take on a different meaning in your life after your experience?

LANDRY: Yes, entirely. I heard many sermons before that meant nothing to me, but now I have understanding , and the Spirit is there. I discovered that when I would read the Bible, something would come over me—I know now it was the Holy Spirit—and this was before I even realized what the gospel was. I didn't realize what was happening, but I was looking forward to that study on Wednesday morning. I didn't know yet what it was, because I hadn't yet realized that one must make a commitment to Jesus Christ. But I knew something really good was happening to me that hadn't happened before.

ANTHONY: I've heard it said that seventy-five percent of the people in the world who call themselves Christians have never read the Bible. What would you say to someone like that?

LANDRY: I can't see it. Maybe it is possible, but I can't see anybody being a Christian without the Bible. It would be like my expecting my football team to go out there and play a game without the play book. To me, without the Bible as the guide, I don't see how anybody could be a Christian. If he does have a Damascus road kind of experience where it happens all of a sudden, I don't believe he will keep it unless the Bible is at his right hand all the time.

ANTHONY: The "manufacturer's handbook" as someone has called it.

You know, a man really isn't big enough to handle success until he has Christ, is he?

LANDRY: I think that's true.

ANTHONY: There are many people who handle success in a way that is not complete. What often happens—at least what has happened with people I know—is that the imagination keeps conjuring up more and more things, so that completeness is not possible. Maybe if we used words like "complete" instead of "saved"—words the world can understand—we would be more effective.

LANDRY: Sometimes I feel maybe I am too simple in my witnessing, but I feel that God who created this world and created people—many of whom cannot understand theological language—is best explained in simple terms. I think the gospel is simple. Not that we shouldn't mature, but we should be simple. When I get a hang-up, then I bring Christ back into focus and everything seems to right itself. But as long as He is at a distance and I am trying to wrestle with these theological questions, I have a lot of problems. It may sound naive, but it's true to my experience.

ANTHONY: The natural mind cannot understand the things of the Spirit, so if we are going to approach men who do not have Christ, we must speak to them in terms they can understand.

Tom, do you believe in prayer?

LANDRY: Yes.

ANTHONY: I wonder if we really understand what prayer is.

LANDRY: I thought your illustration at our Bible group recently was good. Prayer is like planting a seed. After you plant a seed, you don't go back and dig it up. You just let it be and let it grow. Until we grasp that concept, we keep praying over and over for something, instead of realizing that once we've asked God for something, the seed has been planted, and we have nothing more to do.

ANTHONY: We're sure that a watermelon seed is going to turn out to be a watermelon, even though we can't see anything. Yet we often don't have faith in God's Word. Jesus told his disciples not to pray repetitiously, because the Father in heaven knows what we need even before we ask. In some ways, prayer is just an affirmation of what we are asking for, and we are in an attitude of agreement with God. The Lord expects us, and has told us, to pray for the desires of our hearts. So we can have whatever we ask in His name with authority. Can you imagine the authority we could have as believers, as sons of God, if we would only accept it? It is the attitude that is really important.

Tom, I wonder how it must feel to realize you have to "walk the talk" before several hundred thousand people each week, when you are under tremendous stress and pressure. The commentators are always looking at you, and I can just imagine them asking, "Is he living the life when that person misses the field goal that was going to mean the winning points?" Or in 1967 in Green Bay, "Was he living the life when the Cowboys just missed becoming the world champions?" That must be an interesting challenge!

LANDRY: It really is, Ole. So often reporters will ask me, "How do you live the Christian life? How do you do things differently in front of so many people and on the sideline?" Until they started asking the question, I really hadn't thought about it, because I think a Christian is a Christian, regardless of what he is doing—whether he is coaching a football team or whatever. I was never conscious whether I was living a Christian life in the eyes of people before they started asking me this question. I always live the life of a Christian to the best of my ability, regardless of what the situation is. And I hope I react as a Christian should react in those situations you mentioned.

ANTHONY: What is the single most memorable experience you've had since you became a Christian?

LANDRY: I remember specifically a couple of Cleveland losses, after we had done so well against the Packers and had played such great games, and almost won that world championship you were talking about, when quarterback Bart Starr sneaked on the last play and we lost. Then we came to a couple of games after that and played Cleveland, where we had had great seasons and were favorites, and we just got bombed in the playoffs. It seemed like the world had come to an end in one football game. But the thing that was so remarkable to me was how quickly I was able to bounce back from that type of defeat. Of course, a football coach doesn't sleep much after a football game. He replays the whole thing and wonders why he did something wrong when he could have done something better. I don't know what other coaches do. But it is great to be able to kneel and ask Christ to help you work things out, so when the sun comes up the next day and you have to face a bank of reporters and the whole truth of the matter, to know He will give you the strength to stand tall. Each time He has put me right back on my feet so quickly, to go right on, to come back—and we've won a few since then.

ANTHONY: How in the world do you keep your cool when you're walking the sidelines when you're being romped? How did you keep your cool in the Minnesota game in 1973? Do you seek the Lord literally during those situations?

LANDRY: I don't think I seek Him at that particular moment. The thing we Christians who are in football try to do is to pray with our team. We pray that we can use the talents God gave us to the best of our ability and for His glory. We know the scoreboard is going to go against us out there sometimes, but we're not really concerned about that. I feel I am in His will to be in football, and I just try to do my best. Even if I had discovered Christ earlier, I'd still be in football because I believe that is where the Lord wants me. Therefore, when these things come I can ride them through, because I know that a single game is not the ultimate in life. I can see how it could be for some people if the Lord was not involved, because if we live in this materialistic world and we don't have God as part of our plan in life, ultimately our goal is to succeed. And if you fail, you've lost it all. But since I have put God first, I can stand steady in those situations.

ANTHONY: Can you honestly expect Christ to help you defeat the Minnesota Vikings? That is not the issue, is it?

LANDRY: No, not really. It never is the issue. But I really believe that He will intercede for us, in that He will give us the power to use whatever ability we have. And that may be good enough to win football games, if we have the ability. People often ask whether I pray to God that we will win. I say "No, I don't pray that we will win. All I want to do is my best. If we have enough ability, then we're going to win." I really believe that.

ANTHONY: One of your players, John Niland, has received a lot of publicity lately. What is your reaction? What has happened to John?

LANDRY: John's life has changed, no question about it. John was a fellow who was wild, and yet he knew what God meant. He should have been on the right track, but he never was. I don't know the details of the experience he had, and how it came about. All I know is that it changed his life. And it not only changed his life, it's changed his wife's life, too. I've never seen them as happy as they are right now. I think it's wonderful.

ANTHONY: What do the other players think when they see a change in someone like John Niland? Do you ever talk to them about it?

LANDRY: No, but I'm sure they react as you expect people to react. They're very skeptical. They didn't feel that anything really happened, just that it was a lot of newspaper talk. But I think that as they see John they begin to see there is a change. I pray that God will continue to bless his life, because he can have a great effect not only on our football players but upon many other people because of where he is in professional football.

ANTHONY: How do you keep from becoming a

"trophy for Christ" though? How do you avoid that?

LANDRY: I think it's a very tough walk for a football coach, because it is so easy for people to criticize you. I try to do it by example. I would love to be able to speak on a personal note with my players, but I can't because I'm the coach. Therefore, when I see the influence of a Christian athlete, I'm thankful for it.

ANTHONY: But what I mean by being a "trophy for Christ" is the problem of having people look at Tom Landry and see Tom Landry, rather than seeing Christ in Tom Landry. Yet the Lord tells us to be humble. How do you do that?

LANDRY: Well, I don't know how to do it. I have to put that in the Lord's hands. I think the Lord has been able to use me in this capacity where people can see Christ in me, instead of seeing me as a football coach for the Dallas Cowboys. I think He has been able to use me that way. If I didn't think He was using me in that way, I would not make the appearances I make. If I ever feel they are exploiting Tom Landry instead of seeing Jesus Christ, then I won't do it. That has to be in the Lord's hands.

ANTHONY: I don't want to put you on the spot, but do you ever think about it? Do you ever wake up in the morning and say, "Well, how can I be humble today?"

LANDRY: No, not really. Humility is just God in us through Jesus, and He just uses us. It's something that I never worry about. I figure if I am exploiting Tom Landry, then I'm going to get some pricks of conscience someplace. But as long as I'm not conscious of it, then I feel that the Lord is using me.

ANTHONY: Do you resent the "ice man" kind of image? I've known you for about a year, and I've never seen that image; I've always seen a friendly, warm person. I see all those cartoons that the *Times Herald* makes up about you and the "ice man."

LANDRY: It bothers me some. I don't like to think that I have no sense of humor, that I can't appreciate humor, or that I have no emotion. But unfortunately, I am very involved on the sideline. It's because of the nature of the offense and the defense we play that I must continually be engrossed in what is going on. I have to be way ahead of what's happening. And when you concentrate that hard, you lose the emotional end of it. I think that is a good quality to have on the sideline.

I think Ben Hogan was probably the most unemotional man who ever played golf. But no player was ever able to concentrate like Ben Hogan could. And that is probably what made him the greatest golfer of all time. I think concentration in athletics is essential to success. I've developed the power to concentrate because of that. If I wasn't concentrating, I could be as emotional as heck.

ANTHONY: Are you emotional during training camp? I'm visualizing the kind of training camp where I've seen coaches just chew everybody out. Is that how you act?

LANDRY: No, I'm not that type of coach. I don't chew people out, but they know when I'm upset. I don't show that type of emotion with players. Every once in awhile I may lose my temper a little bit, but when I do, they usually know I am really mad!

ANTHONY: You know, success is not in doing, but in *being*. Whether it is being coach of the Dallas Cowboys, or whether it's something else, the ultimate success is not in our counting or knowing how many we have won to the Lord. It won't be measured in ways by which men usually measure success. But it will be whether we, inside, have the witness of the Spirit of Jesus Christ that we are and have been exactly what He wants us to be. It is not up to us to be successful; it is only up to us to be faithful. But that requires honesty. What does all that mean to you in your life, Tom? What is honesty? Is honesty just laying it all right out there?

LANDRY: This is pretty hard, Ole. Honesty is something you can feel in a man. It's amazing, when you're with people very long, all of a sudden you can measure a man's integrity and honesty. You know it's there, and then you don't ever question him. Now, how does that come about?

I really don't know, except maybe it's in performance. We are called upon to perform in honesty and in truthfulness, and when we do it consistently, we take on the type of integrity that we're talking about.

ANTHONY: Have you ever been really burned by people who came to you in the name of Christ in business deals, etc.?

LANDRY: Yes, I've been disappointed in people. I'm constantly called upon because people know I'm a Christian, and therefore the opportunities are so great to go everywhere in the name of the Lord.

Sometimes I think about what Jesus said when He reprimanded the disciples when they said, "This man is speaking in your name," and of course they didn't want him to. But Jesus said, "If he's speaking for me, then he is not against me." I tend to take that position. I don't really consider the motives behind it until they prove themselves one way or the other.

ANTHONY: What about business situations, though? Have you ever stopped to think how many business deals Tom Landry has been offered?

LANDRY: No, but I think in that case you've got to protect yourself. Whenever you're presented a business deal, then you have to use all the knowledge and all the resources you have to determine how good that deal is. There are many people, who, if they offered me a business deal, I would take it on their word. I wouldn't even question it.

ANTHONY: What about things like involvement with

religious organizations? I know you're chairman of the board of the national Fellowship of Christian Athletes, but what about all the others? I am sure you must be offered a lot of things.

LANDRY: This is very difficult. I am a little bit naive as a Christian, because I believe in people who say they are Christians. Whether they are or not is for the Lord to judge; I don't try to judge them. But I have to be careful, because in my position, I would hate to be identified with something that proved to be wrong, or to be against Jesus. It would be a reflection upon the lives of those who look up to me. That's the thing that worries me more than anything.

ANTHONY: Does it happen to you?

LANDRY: Sometimes it does. Sometimes I get into situations, and after I'm in them, I realize I shouldn't be there. But I learn each time.

ANTHONY: What about the situation of someone going around saying, "Well, I'm more of a Christian than you are." I'm thinking in terms of organizations.

LANDRY: I think the Lord has a lot of avenues to reach the people. Many religious organizations have tremendous merit. I think Campus Crusade and their four spiritual laws and their hard-hitting approach is excellent for some people. I think the Fellowship of Christian Athletes' program, which is more a fellowship commitment type of ministry, has an appropriate spot in God's work. Therefore we must be careful that we don't condemn an organization that is working effectively in its field. Sometimes we have to reach out for the Lord through social involvement, because it's pretty hard to make a Christian out of a hungry man. Therefore, the Salvation Army or any group that works in this area can have a great ministry for the Lord. The ultimate is what we're after, and that's life in Christ.

I see so many churches criticize other churches because they don't believe exactly the way the other group thinks they should. But if they're reaching their people with the life of Christ in their way, let's not condemn them. Let's just praise the Lord that they are there and reaching those people.

ANTHONY: I had one of the metropolitan directors of Campus Crusade on the program recently, and I asked him if he could imagine the apostle Paul hopping around the continent of Asia with their tract, the four spiritual laws. He nearly fell out of his chair! But again, each person and organization is different. Christ didn't make us robots. He wants us to be just as we are, yielded to His Spirit, and alive and free. Some of us don't understand that and we get into bondage.

What about politics? Have you ever lent your name to a political candidate?

LANDRY: I am interested in politics, and I have endorsed a candidate, but I haven't allied myself with either political party. I think of myself as an independent, because I will vote for Democrats as well as Republicans. Recently I've been a little more on the Republican side. I've been reading about Harry Truman and I've been getting a completely new insight into the kind of man he was. As I read his life, he's become a favorite of mine, because he had integrity. I think this is a great quality in a person, especially in light of the things happening in this country today.

ANTHONY: I'm sure you have heard of Charles Colson, who was head of the "dirty tricks" department. He recently came to the Lord in a fantastic, beautiful way. It was through Senator Hughes and Senator Hatfield. They got him to come to a prayer breakfast and he accepted the Lord. There are all kinds of little secret prayer groups meeting in Washington that I found out about while I was up there recently. It's almost like an underground thing. Senators and congressmen and White House and government officials are meeting all the time and totally committing their lives to Jesus. You don't hear a lot about it, but I saw evidences of it throughout Washington. Going to a prayer group brings the church down to the reality of praying for one another and sharing one another's problems.

LANDRY: That is the way I became a Christian. Our fellowship on Thursday mornings means a lot to me. I've seen men in our church really become Christians through fellowship and study of the Bible. Unless you use the Bible, I don't know how you could ever stay with a commitment to Christ, or grow.

ANTHONY: What does spiritual growth mean to you?

LANDRY: Well, in football we say that's experience. As we learn more and become more experienced in football, we grow. And I believe it's the same way in Christianity. Most of us, if we had had knowledge of the Bible, would have become Christians a long time ago. We really don't know very much, but as we get into the Bible we learn and become more experienced, then we have growth. There is probably more to it than that. There are Christians who seem to be way out of range of me already in Christian growth, but we grow in certain degrees and we grow as we study.

ANTHONY: Paul says something in Romans that seems ridiculous. He says, "We glory in tribulations also: knowing that tribulation worketh patience; and patience, experience; and experience, hope: And hope maketh not ashamed" (Romans 5:3-5). You must see this constantly, Tom. I can imagine how you must have felt when, from a secular standpoint, it seemed like everything was lost. It seems that these things really show up in an athlete's life.

LANDRY: They really do. You know the old cliché, that you're building character in the losing season. We probably overdo it, and we hear it so much. But that passage of Scripture you read is probably one of my most important passages. The thing I see in athletics—and I think it is true in anyone's life—it is pretty hard to build character without adversity and tribulation. To me, this is why athletics are so important to building character in young people, and why it is so important for them to have a chance to have defeat and to have victory.

I know the Cowboys have gone through many, many difficult years of building character. We've had the two Green Bay championship games that we lost in the last minute of play. We had humiliating defeats by Cleveland that brought the wrath and criticism of many people upon us. These kinds of situations are times for soul-searching. We're in a glass house too, as it were, and that makes it worse. People often ask me, "How can you go out and lose a game—like in 1970 to the St. Louis Cardinals 38-0 on Monday night—and then come back and win and end up at the Super Bowl?" After suffering such a humiliating defeat, most people would quit under the criticism. Most of the time, we couldn't have gone on without the experiences we had had before. The reason we were able to turn around then was because of the adversity we had gone through. The patience and endurance we had developed enabled us to go through these tough times.

We must learn to go through some of these things and develop some character and a hope. I think hope is one of the most important words we have. But once you've gone through this cycle that Paul is describing, and you've developed a character and developed a hope, then you believe that God's plan is going to come about.

ANTHONY: The rest of the passage says, "And hope maketh not ashamed; because the love of God is shed abroad in our hearts by the Holy Ghost which is given unto us" (verse 5). That is a powerful statement.

There are so many people who know so much about

Christ, yet they don't pray. They don't believe the Lord is alive today. They think we're just supposed to know about Him, but not know Him. And that is really sad.

LANDRY: Yes, it is. I remember J.B. Phillips, in his book *Your God is Too Small*, stated that so many people are afraid to really open up the Scripture to see what it says. They feel if they don't know what it says, then they will escape. I think many people are that way; they don't really want to know what is going to be demanded of them.

I am a football coach, and discipline means a great deal to me. But I don't think anyone is more disciplined than a Christian. When Christ asked us to "take up our cross" He was asking us to do a great deal of disciplining.

ANTHONY: He said to follow Him would cost us our lives.

LANDRY: Many people are a little bit afraid of the discipline, but the reward is so great! There's nothing to be afraid of.

ANTHONY: That same God, that same Jesus is alive today. He is in our hearts. When one who doesn't know Jesus thinks of taking up the cross and following Him, he thinks it is necessary to do it in his own strength. He knows himself, and he knows he cannot do it. But Christ gives to us the faith and the strength that is required of us to follow Him.

BEN KINCHLOW

Someone once wrote that most Christians want to live their lives within the sound of a church bell, sharing and fellow-shipping one with another. Ben Kinchlow, on the contrary, wanted to spend his life one foot from hell. For several years he followed the teachings of Elijah Muhammad, Malcolm X and the Black Muslims, then he too had this life-changing experience and he opened himself up to God. Things really started to happen in his life. Ben is a big guy, over six feet tall and with a third degree black belt in karate. But when you look at him what you see is love for his fellowman.

CHAPTER 4

BEN
KINCHLOW

Don't preach to this black man unless you are willing to take me into your house just like I am.

ANTHONY: The Bible says in Romans, "Moreover, we know that to those who love God, who are called according to His plan, everything that happens fits into a pattern for good" (Romans 8:28). That's a heavy statement. *Everything that has happened fits into a pattern for good.* It sort of takes the sweat out of our lives. And I think that Scripture probably means everything that happened even before we met Jesus, because He knows . . . and He knew a long time ago.

Our guest is a testimony to the fact that everything that happens is for good. Our guest is Ben Kinchlow, who was involved in the black power movement and was a follower of Malcolm X and the black power activities of the late sixties. He decided he was going to get an education so he could fight the system and take control. But all of a sudden a miracle happened. He found out Who really is in control. And now his life is devoted to sharing that life that was found in Christ. Ben, do you think you were looking for truth in all the movements you were in?

KINCHLOW: Frankly, I don't believe truth is really what I was looking for.

ANTHONY: What was it, then?

KINCHLOW: What I was looking for was a nebulous

thing. I really didn't know if truth was the answer. I kind of fell for that question that Pilate used on Jesus—"What is truth?" If somebody had hit me in the face with it, I wouldn't have been aware that that was what I was looking for. But I do know I was looking for something I didn't have. And since in this country materialism dictates whether or not you're anybody (if you've got money, you're somebody) I thought success—or, bluntly, having what the white man had—was the answer and was the truth, per se.

ANTHONY: Was it a search for freedom? Is that really what people are looking for?

KINCHLOW: I really didn't know what freedom was. There were some indignities that I would have liked to have escaped, and there were some things that actually weren't necessary. I felt if I could get away from those things, this was what I was after. But as far as being free—I really didn't know what "being free" meant. What I wanted was to escape the pressure; get away from somebody telling me what I could or could not do. And the term that came to mind was "freedom."

ANTHONY: Do you know what "free" is now?

KINCHLOW: Oh, man—I tell you . . . . The verse that really stands out for me is John 8:31,32, which says: "If you continue in my word, then are ye my disciples indeed; and ye shall know the truth, and the truth shall make you free."

ANTHONY: Let's start at the beginning. How did it happen? How did you come to know the Lord?

KINCHLOW: I joined the Air Force with the specific intent of staying in for at least thirty years. There wasn't anything else happening. My parents couldn't afford to send me to college, and at that time the talent scouts were not scouring the black high school campuses looking for athletes as they are now. I decided to go into the Air Force because in the Air Force I discovered if someone didn't like me just because I was black, that was all right. But he couldn't overtly *do* anything about it.

ANTHONY: You didn't have to ride in the back of the bus or anything?

KINCHLOW: Not on a military bus. If you were downtown that was a different story, but on the military bus we all got to do our own thing. I remember one incident in Louisiana. I had just been stationed in Shreveport, and I didn't know much about the city. There was a barber shop on the post right behind my barracks. In the military you are required to get a haircut every so often, so I went in there to get a haircut. The guys all looked at me so strange and I said, "I came to get a haircut." The guy said, "I'm sorry, we don't cut your hair here. You'll have to go on the other side of the post to get your hair cut." I went to the other side to the main PX, and believe it or not—on an Air Force base, a government installation—they had this barber shop that you walked into, and the shop came together at the back. There was another little door you had to go through, and on behind was the place for blacks to get haircuts. These kinds of things stick to you and they feed your resentment. You know, we were all boiling over with resentment anyway, and the least little thing would feed it. And it just so happens that black people's resentments are usually uniform. All blacks have what you might call a corporate experience. We all suffer the same indignities.

ANTHONY: Well, how did it happen? Did you grow up in church?

KINCHLOW: Yes. My mother was a good Christian lady. My dad wasn't such a good Christian, but he was a good man. He didn't come home and beat his wife or beat me up or anything. My mother worked as a schoolteacher, so I got passed around from aunt to aunt around the corner. But in the military, I began to travel around at the expense of the government and I saw lots of things. One of the outstanding things I discovered was that the black man is not in the minority. It's really the white man that is in the minority. In this country you've got inverted vision and you can't really see that.

But I got overseas, and all these things were building up. It all came to a head about the time they were having the explosions in Little Rock, Arkansas. I saw this on television while I was overseas and it really upset me. The newsreel showed the military people standing around with their guns, and the enemy was eight black children trying to get into an American public high school. This brought it to a head, in addition to the things which were already eating at my own personal dissatisfaction. So I decided, "The thing for me to do is to get out and go fight the real enemy—Whitey." By then the Muslims were real strong on the scene and they were gaining national prominence. And Malcolm X was *the* Muslim. The Muslims never would have made it if it hadn't been for Malcolm X. He was one of the most dynamic people I ever saw. I read about and followed his life and I became, naturally, infatuated with him. I wanted to find out what he had. And he was telling us all the time: "Man, I'll tell you what I've got. I've got Elijah Muhammad. I've got the true religion. All you blacks fooling around with this Christianity jazz ought to wise up. Get out of that garbage, man, and come to the real religion."

He said, "You're going to fight somebody. All you stupid blacks in the military—get out of there. That's dumb. Don't go fight somebody who isn't doing you any harm; come back and fight the man who's killing you."

ANTHONY: That's pretty strong.

KINCHLOW: Yes, and it is hard to resist, especially if you have a first sergeant from Tennessee or Mississippi or someplace like that. You go in the NCO club and somebody gets up and leaves the table where you're at, or the veiled

insults you get. Then they tell me, "We're here to defend
democracy and freedom." Well, for who? I haven't got it.
What do you mean, defend democracy and freedom? So I
thought the thing for me to do was to go back home and
fight Whitey if I was going to fight. But if I'm going to fight,
I'm going to fight like Whitey fights. I learned this from
Malcolm X. At this time there were a lot of people going
around shouting, "Black power, black power!" Malcolm
said, "Man, you can holler 'black power' all you want, but
until you get some green power you're just whistling up a
tree. No kind of power gets anywhere without green
power."

So I felt the thing for me to do was to go back and go to
college and to do it like the white man does it. You can't
argue with success, and one thing the western white man
has been is successful. You can't argue with that, and that
was for me. If I was going to fight, I was going to fight like
he fights—paying people under the table and hiring somebody to do my dirty work while I walk around with my
halo. All that *marching* was fine for those people who really
were committed to that; I thought, "That's cool." But
somehow I couldn't see the logic in marching to this guy's
restaurant and *insisting* that he take my hard-earned
money. He didn't even want me to give it to him. He said,
"I don't want your money; get out of here." But I said, "No,
you've got to take my money whether you like it or not."
And so for giving him my hard-earned money, I was going
to get beat on the head with an ax handle. I said, "No, that
doesn't make sense to me. We're going to do it the other
way. I'll go through college and get my degree, then come
out and go to work in the white man's business. Then I'll
know what he knows, and I'll do it like he does it."

ANTHONY: Then you'll turn the knife.

KINCHLOW: Sure, it's a lot easier, man, to insist that
someone do something when you're talking from behind a

big walnut desk with five or six hundred thousand dollars behind you. People have a tendency to listen to that, but they very seldom listen to the poor Mississippi cotton farmer marching down a dusty road in Mississippi singing, "We shall overcome." Well all that's cool, and maybe that's necessary, but that wasn't my bag.

What happened was, I got to a point intellectually where I began to question, "What's the difference?" Because the whole point behind the Muslims is "Hate Whitey." They said, "You must hate Whitey, because look what Whitey has done to you because he hates you." So somehow that was supposed to equal out. If I hate him, then that compensates for his hating me. It got to the point where I couldn't see the difference between the Ku Klux Klan and some of the more militant black movements. They hate and we hate, so what was the difference? While I agreed emotionally with the idea of "Let's go out and fight injustice," intellectually I couldn't reconcile blank, blatant, open hatred. Because if I hate, that gives him the right to hate. All these things were turning in me at once, and I really didn't have anything else to hold onto except the Black Muslims, Malcolm X and the karate. I began to get into that.

My world began to crumble and fall apart, and there just weren't any answers. I could look at a cowboy going across the campus with his big hat on, wearing his boots, getting into his pickup and spinning off his tires—I could resent that. But that only added to the churning and dissatisfaction that was going on inside my own life.

ANTHONY: How did you find Jesus?

KINCHLOW: I met a white guy. I was teaching karate at Southwest Texas Junior College in Uvalde as part of their physical education program. The guy they assigned to be my assistant was a brown belt in judo. If you know anything about the Japanese martial arts, it really can get into a big ego trip. You walk around just looking for boards to jump out so you can go "Ahh!" I got into this really egotistical thing. When you come out to greet a higher ranking belt, you must bow to this belt. There are all kinds of symbolism in this. The very beginning belt in all the Japanese martial arts is white, and the top belt is black. You start at the bottom which is white, and work all the way up, and the next to the highest is brown. And then you go on up to black. And of course when you come in, you've got to bow a certain way to a master, who is your higher rank, and I was a third degree black belt. You have to bow down with the eyes toward the ground and your hands down at your side in a position of absolute surrender: "I acknowledge you as my superior." If you bow to an equal you keep your eyes on him, so in case he starts something you can defend yourself.

But this man had something that I had never seen in anybody's life. I was young and ambitious. I was on the dean's list and I was in *Who's Who* and I was president of my class and I was a third-degree black belt on a small country town campus and everybody knew it.

ANTHONY: You were a big daddy!

KINCHLOW: Yes, the proverbial big man on the campus. I was older than most of my professors, so they couldn't run any jazz down on me, you know. I got to the point where I controlled the classes, because most young kids don't say much in college. I'd go in and if I felt like it I'd say, "Well, today we'll talk about such and such a thing." The professor would come out with his little thing and I'd say, "Hey, that's cool." Then I'd break it all around and the next thing you knew we'd be talking about what I wanted to talk about. One of my favorite tactics was to lean on him racially. In other words, "If you don't go the way I want to go, man, it's because you're prejudiced." And right away he goes my way.

But this guy who was my assistant in karate class was a minister of a small town church in a denomination I never even heard of called the Christian Missionary Alliance. He had a little country church with about twenty members in his congregation and they were all old people. He didn't have anything going for him. He was a little insignificant-looking dude, an Irishman with a big, red nose. But the guy had something. He was peaceful inside. One of the things they teach you about karate—you should have this real deep-down peace. Well, I didn't have this real deep-down peace, and he did. And I was a higher rank than he was, so I was supposed to have it.

I thought, "Well, that's all right. He's lazy; he just doesn't want anything. That's why he's peaceful; the cat is just too dumb to know better. He doesn't even suspect there's anything going on in the world."

One of the things I learned from Malcolm X is that you don't play fair. While you're talking to a guy, you're taking out a knife and going for the underbelly. While you're setting a guy up here and he's reaching for the bait, you get him out there on the limb and you cut the limb out from under him. And Malcolm said, "Practice it at every opportunity." So here this guy was, man. He didn't suspect anything. So I thought, "Well, I'll just practice a little on him before I get to the top. Because when I get up in the big time I'm going to have to know how to smile at white guys and look them in the eye while I'm cutting their throats." And you can't feel guilty. So I thought I would just practice on this guy.

So I cut him with some of the little tidbits of black history that I'd picked up, and I reamed him out about what a bunch of hypocrites the Christians were. And he had no defense, because the Christians have really done a job on their own religion. I'd hit him with jewels like, "Man, if your white brothers don't let me in church with them on Sunday, how am I going to stand all eternity with them in heaven? Somebody's putting me on." And this rage—it was self-manufactured, but it was rage nevertheless—would begin to build up and pour out until I would be shouting and pounding on the table. And this guy—after we would get through all that he would grab my hand and shake it and say, "I'll see you tomorrow."

The next day I'd try to hit him a little harder, because I was going to get him one way or the other. One day I was really pounding on the table—and I was almost hurting myself a little bit by this time—and I saw some water begin to form in his eyes. And I thought, "Wow! I've got him now." But the more I carried on the more I noticed that there was a difference. You see, the guy wasn't hurting for himself or for white folks. He was hurting for me. He was not hurting for blacks in general. He wasn't hurting for injustice per se. He was hurting for *me*, because this guy really cared about *me*.

Well, I couldn't stand it. I just couldn't take that. It really began to freak me out. It just got to the point where I couldn't handle it anymore, so I asked him, "Hey man, tell me, what is it? What have you got in your life?" And he said, "Jesus Christ."

I said, "Oh, no! Oh, no, man! I thought you had something!" I thought this guy had spent twelve or fourteen hours at a stretch standing on his head and eating sunflower seeds or something and going, "Ummmmmm." Something that he had really put some effort into. Then he comes out with, "Jesus Christ."

You see, my daddy had gotten converted while I was in high school and become a preacher. So I had heard all about it. I'd gone to Sunday school and seen pictures of this sad-faced white guy with long hair hanging down and a bunch of little white kids gathered around Him. This was in a black Sunday school, mind you, and He had all these pretty white kids gathered around Him. That didn't say anything to me!

So when he said, "Jesus Christ," I blew it all. And I went on looking for answers in the same old garbage cans. My wife and I began steadily to like each other less. We weren't seeing that much of each other because I worked all night and went to school all day, and she worked. And the times we were together all we did was cut each other up and yell and scream at each other. My kids were getting paranoid. When I would walk out the door they'd run up and say, "Are you coming back, Daddy?" They never knew. It was really getting bad.

Yet, by all the standards that I had set for myself, I was making it, man. I was making close to one thousand dollars a month while in school. For me, a country boy, without being through college or anything, that was a lot of money. It's still a lot of money, one thousand dollars a month. But I thought, "Boy, I'm really making it, man. I've got a new car and I'm big man on campus and I'm making almost a grand a month, and I'm on my way to the top." What can you do to stop me? You couldn't stop me. But inside, man, inside I hated myself. Because hate is like a cancer. It doesn't stay in one place, it spreads through. In my confusion I was wondering, "How can I hate these white people when there's somebody like John, and the counselor, and the guys I know at the college?" They were just nice, country guys. And I thought, "I'm supposed to hate these jokers!" And here I am talking to Dean Underwood and shaking his hand and the guy is bending over backwards to see what he can do for me to help me to get a scholarship. Yet I'm supposed to hate the dude. And while I hated the injustice, I couldn't hate him. So the confusion was tearing me apart.

Finally it all came to a head. My wife was working, and I came home from school and just said, "Well, this is it." I borrowed a guy's pickup and came in and grabbed my king-sized bed and boogied on out the door. I went over and found me a place in another city and decided that was the end of it. I didn't care about my kids; I didn't care about my wife. My parents were living right there in town and it just tore them up. Her parents were all torn up about it. Everybody was torn up. And I was torn up about it. But I couldn't stand it anymore.

Finally late one night I was driving around in a test car at eighty miles an hour on a test track. The radio was blaring and I was singing one of the latest hit songs. I stopped singing this hit song, and the next thing I knew I was singing a hymn. I said, "Oh, come on, man." I turned the radio up a little louder and started singing a little louder. I sang a few lines and the next thing I knew I was singing that hymn again. I turned the radio full volume and rolled down the windows and began to shout out into the night, but before I had gone a quarter of a mile I was singing that hymn again. The title was, "My Heavenly Father Watches Over Me." I stopped and thought back to all the times when by rights I should have been dead. I thought about it and said, "Yeah, He really does." Then I said, "If You're up there . . . I mean, if You're really into anything . . . " I told him, "I can't take any more of this religious garbage. Don't give me any of that religious junk. If You've really got something to offer, I want it. If You don't, leave me alone."

Let me tell you, man, God heard that prayer. It wasn't put in flowery language. But if you go to God with a heart that is really seeking Him, He hears that. And He came into my life right there on the test track at eighty miles an hour, and that's dangerous! I almost ran off the road.

ANTHONY: Our testimony must be that if the Lord can save me; if He allows me to enter into His Life—the sinner that I was, and the rottenness I was—there isn't anyone in the world that He cannot save.

Let's talk about your experiences growing up in south Texas as a black. I had one experience in my life when I can honestly say that I was a victim of prejudice. I was the lone white reporter in a Black Muslim conference. For about three or four hours I sat in the midst of that group, hearing the words of Christ, Muhammad—they just take whoever is handy, whose words meet with their preconceived notion of religion, mix them all together and you've got Black Muslim—at least that is my impression. But I felt prejudice against me. For the first time in my life I was not part of the majority. Now that doesn't happen to most of us. But you, Ben, grew up in a small town in south Texas with all the racial prejudice against you. How did that make you feel? What did you think when you were ten, eleven or twelve years old? What did you think about yourself? Did you think you were less than others?

KINCHLOW: No, I was born in a town which didn't seem on the surface like it was in the South. I really didn't know what prejudice was until I graduated from the eighth grade. I knew what it meant to be segregated; I knew what discrimination meant. But I didn't know what prejudice meant. Most young children don't really know what that means. I went to school at the school closest to my house, and I went to school with my friends. To me, it made absolutely no sense to go all the way across town to go to school with a bunch of kids that I didn't know. I was comfortable where I went to school. I liked the fact that all my friends were there. It was great. We used to laugh at the Mexican kids who lived all around our school who had to walk ten or twelve blocks away to go to school! They had to leave earlier than we did, and they couldn't come home for lunch, and they had all these hardships on them. And we just lollygagged around and laughed it away.

ANTHONY: You didn't know you were being prejudiced against?

KINCHLOW: No. I thought, "Hey, this is cool." Where else would I go to school? And this went on all through grade school. When we went to the movies we had to go in the balcony. They only had one door into each of the two theaters; but we had to go upstairs after we got in.

ANTHONY: Did that seem strange to you?

KINCHLOW: Well, not really. Because when you get to sit up in the balcony you get to throw popcorn and boxes and stuff down on those poor jerks sitting down below. And not only that, at that time it cost fifty cents to sit downstairs, and you could sit upstairs for forty cents. That gave you an extra dime for popcorn! Why pay the extra dime to sit downstairs and let someone throw popcorn boxes on you?

ANTHONY: When is the first time you remember being conscious of a feeling of discrimination?

KINCHLOW: In the school I went to near my home I only went to the eighth grade. That's as high as it went. Then from the eighth grade we had to move on. Uvalde had a football team, and my dad was *the* football fan. Of course my dream was to graduate and go to high school and become a Uvalde Coyote, to wear the maroon and white and hear everyone singing the fight songs, you know, and hear my dad come out to root for me, "Come on boy, play football!" That's what I was really looking forward to.

Then when I graduated from the eighth grade they came up and said, "Where would you like to go to school?" I said, "Well, that's a dumb question. What do you mean? I want to go to school in Uvalde at the high school. I want to be a Coyote." Then they came up with, "Well, I'm sorry, but you're not going to be able to go to school here. But you can go to school either in Brackettville which is forty miles away, or in San Antonio." Talk about busing! They were going to bus us from Uvalde to Brackettville which is a total round trip of eighty-eight miles every day! I thought, "Hey, that would be cool—get to ride the bus for eighty miles every day!" Of course my parents knew better than that, and they said, "No, we're not going to buy that. You can go to San Antonio to go to high school." After I got over the initial disappointment of not being able to be a Coyote I thought, "Well, my dad can come down there to watch me play football. And besides, I'll be going to a big school in San Antonio."

So here we were, eight black children going to high school eighty-five miles away from home. The funny part about it is that we were costing the Uvalde school board almost twice as much per student to go there as it would have been to send us to school in Uvalde. And that was my first real brush with active discrimination besides guys just calling me the usual names.

When I was a kid we used to have these slingshots. You take a two-pronged thing and put a piece of rubber on it. The white kids and Mexican kids would shoot us with these things. We didn't have any, so we would throw rocks. So for the longest time I thought they were nigger shooters, and that's what we used to call them. But I wasn't a nigger. That didn't mean anything to me. I knew who I was. We used to make up a little rhyme with the white kids and Mexican kids. We would go up to one of them and say, "Hey, you know what?" He'd say, "What?" And I'd say, "You're a nigger and I'm not!" It just didn't register. "Nigger" didn't spell anything to me at that particular time. But as I said, maybe I lived in an unusual town.

ANTHONY: But as you grew older you came up against more and more prejudice?

KINCHLOW: Oh, yes, I began to react. People would tell me, "Hey, man, it's not cool when people call you that. And if you don't do something about it, you're a jive turkey."

ANTHONY: You mean "Uncle Tom?"

KINCHLOW: Well, that came a little bit later.

ANTHONY: You mean "jive turkey" was before "Uncle Tom?"

KINCHLOW: Oh, yes. That's when you're a young cat, you're jive turkey or chicken or something like that. So I began to react to these insults, and I began to see insults where there were none. If somebody would look at me too hard I'd say, "What are you looking at, man?"

ANTHONY: You're a big guy. Did you use your physical strength against Whitey?

KINCHLOW: No. At the time I guess I was basically a coward. I really didn't like the thought of fighting and carrying on.

ANTHONY: When did you start to like it? Intellectually you like it, because you liked what Malcolm X was telling you.

KINCHLOW: Yes, that's true. People intellectually accept war.

ANTHONY: Is that why you went to college, so you could get somebody else to fight?

KINCHLOW: Of course, man. This made sense. This is the way Malcolm X did it. That's why I learned karate. Because I figured if I really knew karate, then I wouldn't have to fight anybody. Karate, if it is exercised properly, is one of the dullest ways to fight. All it is, if it is done right, is when one guy takes a swing, you step inside and break the guy's arm, put out an eye, or crush his larynx, and that's it. Just one punch. All this stuff they show you on television is a lot of malarkey.

ANTHONY: You're black; I'm white. We just met tonight. What do you feel about me? Do you see my skin? What do you feel?

KINCHLOW: Well, because you confess Christ, I feel just exactly toward you the way I feel toward my flesh and blood brother who has also accepted Christ, and who is also my brother in Christ now. You see, it is no longer a matter of what you are; it is who you are. You are in Christ.

ANTHONY: Then it's position?

KINCHLOW: That's right. And that makes you and I one. I mean literally, it makes me a part of you. And when you hurt, I hurt.

ANTHONY: While we've been sitting here tonight I literally forgot that you are black. Do you see what I mean? All of a sudden I found myself thinking, "Hey, he's black!" But it doesn't make any difference, obviously.

KINCHLOW: That's why you say that in Christ there is neither black nor white nor Jew nor Greek nor male nor female. When you're in Christ, I can be talking to a woman and forget she is a woman, until I snap back carnally to the natural man and say, "This is a woman."

ANTHONY: You notice her legs or something . . . .

KINCHLOW: I notice this is a white guy because his hair drops down and he's got blue eyes. But white is an attitude, and black is an attitude. And until you come into Christ there is no way you can separate that.

ANTHONY: I want you to spend a few minutes talking to those who are involved in the black power movements. Pretend I am the local leader of whatever the most militant black liberation group is. But at the same time, pretend I am also the most militant anti-black. You see what I'm saying?

KINCHLOW: Yes, because they are both one and the same.

ANTHONY: They are both bigoted. How would you approach me?

KINCHLOW: First of all, man, you are not really looking to be free. You're not interested in freedom. What you're interested in doing is satisfying something that is missing inside yourself. By hating me, that allows you to look out of yourself and into me. You can forget your own shortcomings, you can forget how raunchy you really are, because you can transfer all of that to me. And no matter how raunchy you are personally, you can always say, "Well, I'm better than that guy right there."

No matter what you're missing you can always say, "Well, I've got more than that. And the reason I've got more than that is because of you, Whitey." Not because you haven't had the opportunity for an education, even in a segregated school. Even in a segregated school you can get an education. But you can say, "Because I haven't hit the books and applied myself, and because I haven't studied and taken advantage of what has been given me, I can blame you, Whitey. And because I haven't really busted my knuckles working to make something out of myself, I can blame you, Whitey." And by the same token, just because you're white, you figure, "Well, I can slide right on through society and don't really have to do anything. Because no matter how sorry I am, I'm always better than you, bigger. So it doesn't make any difference what I do. Because no matter how low I go I am always one step above the nigger because I'm white."

Man, you are the slave, not me. Your black power shouts or your "Down with the blacks" shouts—all those things are bondage, because of what is missing in your own life. If you want to really be free, I'll tell you where it's at. But you're not really looking for freedom, are you? You're not really looking.

ANTHONY: What does Romans 8:1 say?

KINCHLOW: "There is therefore now no condemnation to them which are in Christ."

ANTHONY: You lose the right to condemn yourself in Christ. And once you've stopped condemning yourself, you no longer feel any need to condemn anybody else, whether you're black or white or whatever.

KINCHLOW: It's something I really can't explain. One

of the things I used to dislike about Christians was the fact that Christians were always willing to preach to me. The thing that made an impression on me, though, was this guy, John Corcoran who lived it, and loved me. Man, it was so obvious. And I just couldn't resist that. Because when I hated him and when I spewed out my venom at him, it bounced off of him. As the song says, he could look beyond my faults and see my need.

ANTHONY: It's what Galatians 5:22, 23 says: "The fruit of the Spirit . . . against such there is no law." Nothing can stand against it. It becomes the actual life of Christ in your life, manifested by the Spirit, and there's no law that can stand against you.

KINCHLOW: I think the greatest thing is to be really free. That's why that verse means so much to me. You see, while I was in the service I went around the world, and I forgot. There are some places you can go where people don't look at you as a black, except like you would say, "That's a black cover on that Bible." They will just say, "Well, that's a black man." And oddly enough, in the countries where they didn't believe in God and Jesus Christ—those were the countries where I felt most at ease as a black man.

ANTHONY: That's weird, isn't it?

KINCHLOW: Let me tell you, man—blacks and whites and chicanos, your brown power—whatever it is— there is no freedom whatever outside of Jesus Christ.

ANTHONY: Ben, most of our listeners are Christians who grew up in the church. They are the Christians you hated at one time. What would you say to them?

KINCHLOW: Jesus said to His disciples, "Ye shall receive power, after that the Holy Ghost is come upon you: and ye shall be witnesses unto me both in Jerusalem, and in all Judea, and in Samaria, and unto the uttermost part of the earth" (Acts 1:8). Without the fullness, the actuality of

Christ in your life by what He promised in the power of the Holy Spirit, there is no hope. But I would say this: don't preach to me unless you're willing to take me into your house just like I am.

KEITH MILLER

Keith Miller is author of several books, including *The Taste of New Wine*, *A Second Touch*, *Habitation of Dragons*, and *The Becomers*. On meeting him you see someone who looks like a distinguished corporation executive. When he speaks, he is controversial in many ways, but he is *real*. You may not agree with everything he says in the forthcoming interview, but you will have to agree he makes you think.

CHAPTER 5

KEITH MILLER

Some days I'm so sick of smiling my teeth are dry and I don't ever want to see another Christian.

ANTHONY: Our guest tonight is a man many of you have heard about. Many of you have read at least one of his books. He wrote a book called *The Taste of New Wine* which has been instrumental in starting a revolution in a lot of people's lives and in a lot of churches. Keith, it is nice to have you here.

What else have you written?

MILLER: A book called *A Second Touch*, one called *Habitation of Dragons*, and one called *The Becomers*.

ANTHONY: But *The Taste of New Wine* has been the biggest seller?

MILLER: Yes, it has.

ANTHONY: Although I have read one of your books, I am going to approach this discussion as though I knew nothing about you. When I look at you I don't see a guy who looks like a typical Christian. I don't see a "holiness" aura around you; I see somebody real. What does reality mean in terms of your life?

MILLER: Gosh, you know, I'm not sure. Sometimes it seems to me to be different things. Several years ago I accepted a hypothesis which is more real to me than anything else, and it has helped to shape what I see when I look at the word "reality." But I suppose reality, for me, is that which is in my mind that conforms with what I can touch and check out in the real world.

ANTHONY: How long have you been a Christian? What does it mean when I ask, "Are you a Christian?"

MILLER: Well, it might mean a lot of things, depending on who you are. It means to me that I have decided I am going to give the keys to my future to God as I see Him revealed in the life and death and resurrection of Jesus Christ. I was in the oil business for fifteen years and I was a real skeptic. I've read a lot—although I've tried to hide this because I've been desperately insecure intellectually—but I read all the time. And I've always felt there must be a God. I kept knowing that there must be something more than the things I was finding out. I tried very much to look sophisticated.

ANTHONY: Do you dye your temples gray?

MILLER: No, that just happened as the result of a lot of questions like you're asking me! Life was pretty simple before I became a Christian. All I had to do was say, "Two more, please," and get on with it. But I suppose that being a Christian, to me, means taking God seriously and saying, "All right, my life has been centered in myself. I've always tried to be God in my world, but now I want You to take over." I tried to control my life; I wanted to be famous. I didn't know what I was going to do, but I was going to be big. I was sure of that. This was, I think, because my dad loved my older brother more than he loved me. My dad is dead now, but since the time I was a little kid I felt I had to *be something* in order to win my dad's love. And I never could do enough, even though I am a tremendous overachiever. I paid a tremendous price to get anywhere. And when I finally ran out of gas, I just was heartbroken. I had an awful feeling of no worth.

I turned to God by a roadside in east Texas while I was working for an oil company. I had checked out a company car, and in total despair, I just started driving as fast as I could. I pulled off at the side of the road. It was in August and there was no air-conditioning at that time, and I just sat there sweating by the side of the road. I had always been a self-sufficient kind of guy. But I had no hope anymore.

I remember thinking about God and saying, "Hey, anything You want in my stinking life, take it!" Not because I knew anything about commitment—I'd never known anybody who was a committed Christian who would admit it. It was just that I didn't have any use for my life. That was weird, because I've always been a real optimist. But I just said that, and all of a sudden—I'd like to tell you that lightning struck the hood and Jesus Christ appeared. But that wasn't it. I began to cry and weep. I'd been raised in the southwest and a man doesn't cry, so I'd repressed all this. But suddenly it was all right to cry.

In retrospect, it was the cessation of a conflict of a lifetime. I was trying to prove that I was something, and suddenly it was as if God said to me, "You don't have to prove anything to Me. I love you." I have always felt very unlovable. I always thought if someone really knew me, they would walk away. But I didn't feel that way anymore. My orientation is Episcopalian, and I had never been to an evangelistic meeting. I remember I drove home in a daze and poured myself a tall scotch and water to think it over. Sometimes when I say that now people say, "How could you be a Christian!?" Well, there wasn't anybody there to tell me that God hates scotch or anything like that. I lived as a Christian for four years without telling anyone.

ANTHONY: About the scotch and water, or about God?

MILLER: About God. The scotch and water I wouldn't mind telling. I mean, if you came around at 5:00 it was time. But what happened was, since there wasn't a community around to tell me what I had to believe, I read the Scriptures. I began to ask, "If these principles are true, how do you live them out in business?" I'm sure that is why my books don't have a religious sound, because I didn't get the package deal.

Later, when I met some Christians . . .

ANTHONY: You got a package deal?

MILLER: They said, "Hey, you're not saying that right!" I asked, "How come?" I knew the Scriptures pretty well, but they would say to me, "Jesus didn't say that." I said, "Wait a minute, who said He didn't say that? He ran around with whores and bums and they felt at home with Him. With the kind of language they used, they didn't change that much or they wouldn't have felt at home with Him. Now what kind of a deal are you talking about? They don't feel at home with you!"

Why don't the people who are really sick feel at home with us? They feel at home with me now, and I feel at home with them. And I love them and I love Jesus Christ with all my heart. But my talking like that just blew their minds. They said, "We'll pray for you." I said, "Please do; I really want you to."

ANTHONY: When did this happen?

MILLER: In about 1956. I had been to seminary earlier. I'd lost my parents; everyone died on me when I was very young. I've planned funerals from the time I was young.

ANTHONY: Died on you? That's an interesting way of looking at it.

MILLER: That's right; they had left me, and I was all alone. I broke my neck and thought I was going to be paralyzed from the neck down. As they were dying, they used me as a confessor, because I was the walking case. I realized that I had known these people for years, and we were a close family, a warm family with integrity. But inside, my mother could have changed eight things she was doing in her behavior and transformed my dad's life. And the same way with him. But it was so touchy that they couldn't talk about it to each other.

I thought, "If they are this close, what must the world be like? What must we be hiding from each other?" Suddenly I began to realize that maybe other people are as alone as I am, and afraid of death, and afraid of life, afraid of success, afraid of failure, afraid of all of it. Yet I'd just been looking cool and achieving like crazy to keep people from knowing that inside I was afraid of life. As this began to happen, that is when I started looking. And this led me to go to seminary.

I went back to New Haven, Connecticut, to an Episcopal seminary connected with Yale, and studied. I didn't know anything about theology, but I had a damn fine bunch of questions to ask because I'd just buried a bunch of people.

ANTHONY: You know you just wiped out a whole gang of people. You said, "Damn."

MILLER: Well, those of you who have been wiped out, forgive me. You see, "damn" where I come from is punctuation. It's a matter of language. This is another big hang up. You know, Paul said about the dogs—well, the nicest way I can say it is, "You ought to castrate those people." There is another way to say that that would knock the rest of you out. But we've emasculated the way we read the Scriptures. Actually they're really very earthy.

For those of you who are turned off because of "damn," I wasn't talking to you anyway. I am only interested in the people who understand that "damn" is not a nasty word. I only use it for emphasis. The rest of you are in the ninety and nine and you're in great shape; pray for me. I'm talking to that one guy out there who may really want reality, but because he says "damn" they don't love him down at the church, so he has to hide it. Now God loves people who say "damn." I don't mean to do this in a showy way, but it is only language, and it is effective where I come from. The rest of you—I am just simply not talking to you. I'm sorry if it hangs you up, and I don't want to offend you.

ANTHONY: What do you think about righteousness?

MILLER: Well, I think of it as nearly as I can like Jesus did. He said, "Don't you call me righteous." That is what He said, and certainly He wasn't meaning to deny His divinity. He was saying, "The point is not righteousness. That's God's deal. Only God is righteous." Therefore, the point is *love*. And I can sometimes love you—sometimes. Mostly I just love me. Mostly I hate me and love me. But if I love God, then anything you might call righteousness . . . if I don't con you, that is God's love coming through me.

ANTHONY: And it's real.

MILLER: So you see righteousness is His problem and His deal. I think we've made it ours, and that's pharisaical. If you judge me on how righteous I am, or put me down because I don't talk like you talk, then we can't have fellowship. But if I can talk to you about reality and pain and how God has helped me, and how because of His faithfulness and righteousness I am able to cope and live, then I don't care whether you call me righteous or not. That's your problem.

ANTHONY: If you smoke are you going to hell?

MILLER: How should I know? I'm not God. These are the kinds of judgmental questions we ask each other. I know you're kidding, but if you ask this kind of question and someone says, "Oh, no," or "Oh, yes," that would make him the guy who judges. And you see, I can't answer that kind of question.

ANTHONY: Didn't God say that the fullness of His plan is in His Son?

MILLER: No, He said the fullness of His plan is in His Son if you don't smoke! Don't you see how ridiculous men make God's beautiful plan! The *Life* is *Jesus Christ only*.

ANTHONY: Hey, what happens if you ask God what time it is?

MILLER: I don't know; why don't you try?

ANTHONY: I did. He said, "It's now."

Keith, after you had this experience of coming to know the Lord, what happened in your family life?

MILLER: Well, I suppose my wife and I could have gotten a divorce. We went to church and took the children to church, not all the time, but some. My wife is a very lovely girl; she had been a beauty queen in college and is very intelligent. She thought religious people were kind of kooky, and suddenly she had one in the house and in the bed with her. For three or four years it was all right, because I didn't tell anyone. I was studying and she just thought I was rather quiet. But things were beginning to change, little things. Like, I've always lied a lot just to keep the static down, little lies, you know. And I began to see myself as if I'd been given a new set of eyes. Suddenly I saw that I was totally self-centered. And I really didn't know it before. I thought I had a few problems, but that basically I was a pretty good guy. Suddenly, as God began to get hold of me and I began to study the Scriptures, I began to say, "Golly, Miller, you're totally self-centered." My wife had been telling me this for years and I thought she just thought I was a selfish little kid.

Little things like this began to happen: one day we had a little argument and she said to me, as she had so often, with this almost despairing tone, "Honey, you're wrong." I remember thinking about what she was saying to me and then saying, "By gosh, I think you're right. I think I *am* wrong." She did a double take and then she said, "Wait a minute, wait a minute! Maybe *I'm* wrong."

This may sound like a small thing, but it began something entirely new. Suddenly, I was becoming realistic about my problems. And I'd always been so sensitive when she came close to revealing my ego to me, that I would just chop her to pieces—all in a loving sort of way, you know, by putting her down. But I began to see that I was the problem in our house. She was just amazed. She didn't know what had happened, but she knew that it was good.

But the bad part was when I'd met some Christians a few years later and they said to me, "You need to come and witness." So I would go and tell them what had happened to me. I wasn't sure what a witness was. The first time I ever gave a public testimony was between Billy Graham and R. G. LeTourneau, and I had never heard either one of them. I was scared to death. It was the first time I had ever spoken outside the Episcopal church. They sent me a letter and said, "Your subject is 'My Personal Experience.'" I got there and found out fourteen other guys had the same subject, and I was so shocked to find out I was giving a public testimony.

When I met these Christians they said, "Man, you've got to have a Christian family. You've got to have family altar." Well, my house was already crowded, and I thought they wanted me to build a thing in there, you know. But I thought, "By gosh, they're right." I wanted to be a good Christian and I'm very competitive, so I tried to get my wife converted. I did everything except put tracts in her underwear. I would leave books and things around for her to find. And this just turned her off like crazy. What I was saying to her was, "Listen, I've found this hope, this new meaning. My life is changed; suddenly it's okay to be me."

But what she was thinking when I said that, she told me later, was: "Suddenly your love is conditional on my changing and being something I don't even know how to be. You don't really love me." (We had been married five years and we had had a great marriage.)

And I thought, "How many men have ruined their homes by putting down their wives and trying to con them into becoming Christians?"

ANTHONY: Or wives ruin their homes because of husbands not being Christians?

MILLER: Right. But finally it hit me. I knew if anybody had run at me like that with Jesus Christ I would have really let them have it. So I finally went to her and said, "Listen, honey, I am really sorry. I have pushed you around and manipulated you and tried to change you. And when I married you I didn't sign up to change you, just to love you. I'm sorry, and I hope you can forgive me. I may do it again, but I don't mean it. This just means a lot to me, but you're on your own. I love you, and I'm going to try to be a good husband, but I don't know how to do that."

You know, she became a Christian within two weeks! Because she recognized the change. When you tell someone that they need what you have, suddenly all the "non-O.K." feelings come to the surface, and it's a put-down. And Jesus didn't do that.

ANTHONY: That forgiveness is so beautiful, but it can't be faked. You've got to be honest, don't you?

MILLER: One time I was going to speak to a sweetheart banquet at a big Methodist church in San Antonio. I had to get up very early to drive to the airport to make this thing, so I said, "Honey, would you get up early and fix me breakfast? I've got to get out of here early."

She said, "Fine." But that night our kids were sick. Well, when I get up with the kids, I shake her and wake her up and say, "Don't worry, I'll get up with the kids!"—you know, so she will know I'm doing it. But she doesn't do that; she just gets up quietly. She had been up all night with one of our kids who was sick at her stomach.

The next morning when I woke her about 5:00 she said, "Honey, do you mind if I sleep?"

I said, "I don't mind if you sleep!" And I walked out and slammed the door. I walked in the kitchen and poured some cereal and sat down and started eating. I heard the door open and here she came with her hair all tied up and her robe wrapped around her.

She said, "I'll fix you some breakfast."

I sat there feeling guilty and said, "Oh no, honey, you don't have to fix any breakfast."

She said, "I'll fix you some breakfast!"

I sat over there waiting for my breakfast and all of a sudden I thought about this sweetheart banquet, and how I was going to tell all those people how to love your wife. I thought, "Golly, I can't go with this." So I turned to her and said, "Honey, I've been a real_____." And I told her—we sometimes use words that would offend a lot more of you—I said, "I've been a real so-and-so."

She looked at me and said, "You sure have."

All of a sudden I was furious. She said, "You really meant it, didn't you?"

I said, "Yes."

She said, "Then what are you mad about? I'm just agreeing with you."

I learned right then, if you use forgiveness as a manipulative technique to get the other person to say they're sorry, that is the opposite of Christianity. So I had to learn how to be very careful, if I confessed something, that I wasn't using it. Because I had used everything to manipulate. Forgiveness is a great thing as long as it is real. So is confession, but confession can be used the same way.

ANTHONY: What do you think Christ meant when He said, "It is finished"?

MILLER: I don't really know. For one thing, His earthly ministry was finished. You can read a lot into it theologically. You can say He felt the job of reconciliation was finished as far as His part was concerned. But I don't think that part will wash, because He wasn't finished. He had to go through and come back. So I don't buy that. I think He meant that this was all He could do; it was over. This was the human Christ speaking.

It's just a guess, but I think at this point He may have said to God, "It is finished." It is one of those enigmatic statements that no one will ever really know until we see Him.

ANTHONY: Is your relationship with Christ pragmatic? Does it work?

MILLER: Yes, when I let it. It's like asking, "Does your relationship with your wife work?" In any kind of personal relationship, what do you mean when you ask, "Does it work?" Is it beneficial to me? Does it help me?

ANTHONY: I mean, why should someone listening, after hearing Keith Miller, consider Christ as a viable possibility?

MILLER: I would just say if a person is lonely, or finds that he doesn't like himself very well; if he is desperately tired of holding up a big mask that is smiling when he would like to relax and be who he is; if a person is so compulsive that he can't stop . . . . You see, these are all the things that I am, and because of having committed my life to Christ, He has given me a great deal of help in these areas. For one thing, I never would have told you those things I just said, because I would have been afraid you might use them against me, or you might not like me. But I feel loved now, by God. I've had an awful time with self-hate, but I'm beginning to like myself better because I believe God loves me and I think if He loves me, who am I not to like myself?

ANTHONY: But is God dealing with Keith Miller per se, to make Keith Miller a better person? Or is He dealing with Christ in you?

MILLER: You are asking me questions that only He can answer. I can tell you what it feels like, but if you ask me ultimately whether He is doing it, I may be deluding myself. It comes back to something we said earlier: the more I bet my life on God and the more I pray, the more coincidences seem to happen that fulfill my life and help other people, or that make me more at home in the world and make me love God more. So by taking this hypothesis that God is real, and that Christ loves me, and betting my life on that, then life has become much better. So I would be a fool not to try the hypothesis since it's making life so much better.

ANTHONY: What did Paul mean when he said, "It is no longer I who live, but Christ lives in me" (Galatians 2:20)?

MILLER: Well, again, only Paul really knows what he meant. I can tell you what I think he meant, but I always have to say that. Because I think one of the things Christians have done wrong is to be so dad-gum sure about what everybody meant. I'm not quite that sure. You see, I'm not even sure what *I* mean. I want to love God more than anything, but some days I want to get out of this whole Christian business. Some days I'm so sick of smiling my teeth are dry, and I don't ever want to see another Christian. I don't know if anyone else ever feels that way but that's the way it really is with me.

Now if God can't take my real self, which He has, how can He take my phony self? So when Paul said that I think he was trying to discuss the paradox I have experienced. In one sense, as I try to commit my life to God, I find myself doing and being things that are not necessarily for my benefit. My being here, for example. I am exhausted. I'd rather be anywhere than out talking on a radio program. What do I need a radio program for?

ANTHONY: It might help you sell some books!

MILLER: Well, I hadn't thought about that. If any of you would like to buy my books, please help send a kid to college. But really, the fact is, I've already sold enough books to send them to college. But I find myself coming to the radio program because I felt I ought to come. I didn't even know you guys; I'd never heard your program. But I thought I should come. Some days I don't; I think this is the wrong thing. You say, "Well, how can you tell whether it's God's will or not?"

Let me ask you a question. Is your mother living?

ANTHONY: Yes.

MILLER: If I were to say "damn" on the radio again—which I will not—would your mother be offended?

ANTHONY: No.

MILLER: How do you know that? You answered so quickly. She's not even here.

ANTHONY: Well, if she's the same mother I had one day ago, she wouldn't be offended.

MILLER: But how do you know she wouldn't be, since she's not here to say that? You answered me with great assurance, because you know her. You know her thoroughly. Well, as I get to know God more, then I get to sense His will without having to ask Him.

As I immerse myself in His life in the Scriptures and with other Christians and in prayer, then I get the sense that "Yes, He would want me to do this." That's why the name of the game is to get to know Him, and then be free. I can begin to let my feelings get educated along His lines, and I think that is what Paul is saying. I live, and yet it is not really me, because my perception is more like Christ's now. It used to be that I would have judged you to determine whether I could use you to help me get somewhere, and if I could, then I'd come to your radio show. But if I couldn't use you, I wouldn't have room for you. Or if it was shady, I would see what the options were.

Now, I just said I was dog-tired, and I didn't know if this was a big radio program or what, or whether anyone would be listening or not, and I still don't. But I just felt this was the thing to do, so I said, "Okay, I'll go with these guys."

ANTHONY: Keith, you seem to have a ministry or a purpose, but you seem to be directed mostly to Christians, at least I gather this from reading your book *The Taste of New Wine*. What is your hurt for the people who haven't experienced what you and I have experienced of coming to be known of the Lord? How do you share that?

MILLER: Maybe it was poor communication on my part, but that book was written for people who have not had this experience.

ANTHONY: I had just the opposite impression.

MILLER: Well, you see, everybody in America is under the shadow of the church. We are permeated with a sort of pseudo-Christian ethical whitewash that is a kind of cultural overlay but which has very little to do with Christianity. So there are a lot of people who would say, "Yes, I am a Christian," meaning, "I am a gentleman."

ANTHONY: Or, "Of course, I am an American."

MILLER: Yes, that kind of thing. So I was really writing to those guys, or to guys who got committed to Christ as a child because they were scared spitless by some evangelist when he said, "You're going to go to hell." The last thing they wanted to do was to go to hell, but then they grew up and decided, "I'm not really afraid of hell." So they outgrew Christianity, not realizing that God deals with each growing area of life. The group they've been exposed to only deals with the beginning. So I really was talking to the people who had been turned off by what they consider to be unreality in the church and in people's lives around them. They want to be real, but they still want God. And it doesn't seem conceivable that they could be a Christian and really be authentic, when they look around them.

These are the people I'm talking to. That's why I'm not after those who are already good, solid Christians. I'm not even talking to them. But the amazing thing is, they are the ones who bought these books. A lot of other people have, but . . .

ANTHONY: Do you know who bought the book?

MILLER: They've gone all over. They are in all kinds of languages, and we've been amazed. In the book I've talked about being a business man, being a family man, trying to pray—I've talked in the American business man's milieu. I think we've sold our business culture to all these other countries, and they're getting all our ulcers and hang ups. And because I was talking about problems they have, they suddenly read the deal to see about the problems. Later on, Jesus was just in there.

ANTHONY: If Jesus were here, how do you think Christ, the Anointed One, would view our religiosity? How do you see what we are doing? What about our going to church on Sunday, our prayer groups on Wednesday nights? We have so structured His life to be in a building, we say, "Come here and feel the presence of God."

MILLER: Well, Jesus hit this in a couple of places in His own time, so you don't have to guess about it. One time when He was talking about this (in John 4), He was talking to a gal who had slept with so many men she didn't know which one to rightly call her husband. It's amazing how many sexually oriented stories Jesus rode the parables in on. We've sort of blotted that out, and some of you may be offended—the same group that didn't like the other thing I said. But just check it out. Jesus used earthy, sexual analogies to bring the spiritual truth across. In this particular case, He was talking to a woman at the well. He said, "We're no longer going to worship God down at the temple. We're going to worship Him in spirit and in truth."

So you see, my ministry is to people who are in psychological pain because they're trapped in an unreal world. Because that is what I came out of; that's where God touched me. So I'm knifing through all this other stuff to get to those guys, and there may be only one in a hundred. That's what the parable of the ninety and nine means to me. The lost sheep—I'm shooting for that guy, and the miracle to me is that these other people are listening.

ANTHONY: I know a woman who has come to the Lord, and she has been berating her husband for weeks now. They've been having constant hassles like what you've described. What about this? The woman has had this beautiful experience with the Lord. Her husband thinks she is a nut. He cusses and she tells him that's no good. Whatever he does she tells him, "No, you need to come to the Lord." How does she handle that? What is her responsibility to God and to man?

MILLER: If she were coming to me for counseling I would say, "Look, I don't think the Scriptures make you responsible for having a good home. But you are responsible, under God, for being a good wife. So leave him alone for a minute and ask yourself, being a good wife, "What are his needs that he would like me to meet?" Start listening to him and watching him. Try to meet his needs in a way he can understand. Instead of buying him a Bible, you may need to buy yourself a black nightgown and make love to him more. This would be the most religious thing you could do, because suddenly you are meeting his needs. And you know, it will break that guy's heart.

If you're trying to love him on your own terms, you're not being Christian. God loved us on our terms before we came to Him. So what she should do is try to find out how to be the best wife she knows how to be, and go be that for Jesus Christ's sake. If the husband never comes around, she can still be a successful Christian wife. If she is willing to love him on his terms, I would bet almost anything I have that that guy is going to be deeply touched and will say, "Hey, I don't know if I can buy this, but God really has changed you." And it seems to me she can have an authentic witness.

But we always try to do the religious thing to nonreligious people, and Jesus didn't do that. He healed them where they hurt.

ANTHONY: He said, "Unless one is born again, he cannot see the kingdom of God" (John 3:3). He can't even perceive it. And yet we preach "kingdom of heaven" and "kingdom of hell" and people can't understand it.

MILLER: We always talk about religious things. Jesus talked about broken lives, he used sexual analogies, he used analogies about whiskey businesses. The greatest parable of all where He talked about redemption, He talked about a drunken whoremonger who ran around with his half of his daddy's money! It really disturbs some people when you say that. We've forgotten about the content, because all we use is the abstract meaning. We slap the religious meaning on people instead of telling the story, which is very life-like. Jesus dealt with their *lives*, the newspaper headline stuff. And I suppose if we were to do that from the pulpit we would get crucified, just like He did.

ANTHONY: Let's suppose for a moment of time that Keith Miller was put in charge of all the radio and television stations in America. Would you make them all religious?

MILLER: Oh, no!

ANTHONY: What would you do? How would you use these media to share something?

MILLER: The first thing I would do is to ask whether you'd give me a week to think about it.

ANTHONY: No, you can't do that. You've got to do it now.

MILLER: Then, off the top of my head, I would try to find out what God's will might be by talking to some other Christians who are pros in the field. I'd get the best information I could get, because I don't think God works just like magic. I think He wants us to do our own work.

ANTHONY: I'm talking about gut feelings.

MILLER: Well, I think I would have the radio stations begin to deal with the gutsy issues of life in their programming, and to begin to be very real and very open to try to solve the problems of people who are listening to the station. I'm not talking about just laying a religious solution on them. I'm talking about really trying to help them relate to each other, and dealing with the problems people really have. Begin with that, and begin to find out what the people's problems are; get them to communicate.

ANTHONY: On the one hand we've got legalism, and on the other hand we've got humanism. Both are struggling away, pulling at the Cross. If you end up only trying the "war on poverty" approach, then you have no solution. I was on the board of directors of it for two years, and it doesn't work.

Fortunately, I've never been in on the legalism approach, but it makes me sick to my stomach. If we did what you say, it could become humanistic.

MILLER: No, no. The people who would be doing this would be committed to Christ. This is very important. You see, Jesus hid for three years before he told the people who He was, and He never really did in one sense. He loved them on terms they could understand. They'd never been loved like that by someone who wasn't asking something from them. Then they would ask Him who He was, and He was finally able to reveal it to them, after He had lived it out with them.

So you ask me how I would start? I would start by living the way Christ lived with them, by helping them with their problems as they see them. I would start a dialogue, then when they call and ask, "Why do you do this?" I would have a reason. I would say, "Well, you see, I've been helped." That way they will listen, if *they* ask the question. If you drop the truth on them they run from it, because they don't know if it's birds flying over or what.

ANTHONY: We didn't even talk about the Keith Miller who's a business man.

MILLER: I do some business consulting, but mostly I'm writing, and I do some public speaking.

ANTHONY: Are you writing a book now?

MILLER: Yes, I am.

ANTHONY: What's the name of it?

MILLER: I don't have a name for it yet. I'm doing a book on a Swiss Christian psychiatrist named Paul Tournier. I'm actually doing three books right now. The second one is on how to use personal experience in witnessing and communicating the gospel. This book will deal with how to take your own case history and meld it in without bragging or without offending the people you are dealing with.

ANTHONY: Without glorifying our humility?

MILLER: That's right, without having competitive sinning.

ANTHONY: Is Jesus Christ real?

MILLER: You'd have to ask somebody else if He is for sure, but I would bet my life on it!

ANTHONY: But you'd bet your life on it?

MILLER: Yes.

DEREK PRINCE

Derek is from England, a Greek and Latin scholar, and was formerly a resident professor in ancient and modern philosophy at Cambridge. He is also a student of Hebrew and Aramaic. During World War II on the deserts of North Africa he was converted to Christ. He speaks with authority. Teacher, minister, educator, missionary, an interpreter of what is happening in the Body of Christ, he has a profound and vital impact on those who hear him. This interview took place on the day Richard Nixon resigned and President Ford was sworn into office. A naturalized American citizen, he has some fascinating things to say about what is happening in the U. S. Government.

CHAPTER 6

DEREK PRINCE

God has but one remedy for our old selves. He doesn't make
us better, He executes us.

ANTHONY: Our guest tonight is a man whose books you have perhaps read. His name is Derek Prince, a man who has a particular burden for praying for people in leadership positions in our country. Maybe together we can discern something of what is happening in this country. Derek, do you feel that much more is happening than we see on the surface?

PRINCE: I think the events of yesterday and today are extremely important. I'm sure there are many aspects of them which we don't fully understand, that are hard to assess. But I would have to say that my personal opinion is that God, in a strange way, is answering the prayers of His people. Probably that could seem surprising to many people, and I have to be very careful that I don't hurt anybody's feelings or wound their susceptibilities.

I have to make it plain that I have a British background; I was educated and brought up in Great Britain. I became an American citizen four years ago, and I am proud of it. I think I appreciate America more than do most Americans. I tell people I am an American by choice, not by the accident of birth.

Over the years I have preached the Word of God and served Christ to the best of my ability in many different

countries and situations and backgrounds. One particular
theme which God has emphasized for me since I first came
to know the Lord Jesus Christ personally is the importance
of praying for those who are our leaders, politically,
militarily, and in every area of our lives. I have sometimes
wondered why all Christians don't see the importance of
this. I suppose it is a particular theme the Lord has emphasized for me, but it is one which is clearly emphasized
in the Bible, and that is where I find Christians are delin-
quent.

Paul says in 1 Timothy 2:1, 2: "I exhort therefore, that,
first of all, supplications, prayers, intercessions, and giving of thanks, be made for all men; For kings, and for all
that are in authority." I take those words seriously. I believe our first responsibility as Christians meeting in an
assembly is to pray for our government. This is where I
take issue with the majority of Christians and churches,
because I find they don't do that. They have no conception
of doing it. I think many of the problems which have come
to the United States in the last decade or so are indicative of
the failure of Christians to discharge their responsibility to
pray for their government.

I was in Seattle, Washington, in 1963, the day the
assassination of President Kennedy took place. My wife
and I have a regular practice of praying together during the
morning before beginning the day's activities. There are
times when God gives me what I would call a prophetic
prayer—in other words, something I haven't thought of
previously. I am often surprised to hear myself say it. That
morning, before we had any knowledge of the tragic events
of the day, in our prayer time I said this: "Lord, intervene
in the affairs of the nations." At the time I wondered why I
was saying it.

I feel that from 1963 until today, which has been just
over a decade, there has been a totally new kind of trend

and atmosphere in American politics. I think many secular writers and publications have recognized this. Right at the beginning of that crucial period which was marked so dramatically by the assassination of President Kennedy, I think God showed me He is concerned about what is taking place, that He is not indifferent, that things are not outside His control, but He wants His people to pray intelligently.

I have to say that I am innocent about American politics. I realize there are the two parties, the Republicans and the Democrats, just as there are two major parties in Britain, Labor and Conservative. It may astonish many Americans, but I don't see too much difference between Democrats and Republicans. Really, when it comes to actually doing things, it seems to me that basically they do the same things. You may consider me ignorant or lacking in discernment, but I say that because I really am without political prejudice, as far as I know. I feel the American nation has something to contribute to the world which is not yet fully worked out, and I have had a real concern for the destiny of this nation.

About eight years ago I began to pray, rather systematically, for the government of this nation. It is a very simple prayer: "Lord, raise up the righteous and put down the wicked." In my experience I have discovered that the most effective prayers I pray in this kind of situation are very simple ones. In fact, one of the keys to being effective in prayer in a political situation is to find the right prayer.

Let me digress for a moment. I met the Lord Jesus Christ in a personal way in a military barracks room in the British army in 1941. Shortly afterwards I found myself in the British army in North Africa; I spent two or three years in North Africa. I took part in the longest retreat in the history of the British army, which was a continuous retreat of 750 miles from a place in Tripoli to the gates of Cairo, El

Alamein. I was newly acquainted with God and the things of God; I had no religious background, no church or minister to go to, and I had to work things out for myself.

It so happens that I am the son of an army officer and all my family have been in that military tradition. I was very disturbed by the conduct of the British officers where I was. I thought they were irresponsible and in many ways unworthy, and I knew, as a man serving in the ranks, that they lacked the confidence of the men they led. In many ways they were selfish and self-centered. In the face of this continuing apparent disastrous retreat, I felt a tremendous urge to pray. But I thought to myself, "How can I pray for this kind of leadership?" I really trusted the Lord to give me a prayer that He could answer, and this was the prayer He gave me: "Lord, give us leaders, such that it will be to Your glory to give us victory through them." I prayed this prayer, and God had also taught me directly, without anyone preaching it to me, the importance of fasting as a part of Christian discipline and as a way to intensify the power of our prayers. So I used to fast regularly every week. And in the desert, in the sand and all the rest of it, I prayed, "Lord, give us leaders, such that it will be to Your glory to give us victory through them."

Well, the British government decided to replace the then commander-in-chief in the Middle East, chose another man who was a brigadier serving in the desert. He hadn't been very successful as a brigadier, so why they chose him as a commander-in-chief is something of a mystery. They flew him back to Cairo to take command; his plane crashed on landing and he was thrown out; his neck was broken and he was killed. The situation was critical, but they had no commander-in-chief for the most active theatre in the war. At that point Winston Churchill, acting more or less on his own initiative, chose a little-known commander in Britain named Bernard Montgomery. He was flown out to the Middle East and he was put in command.

Well, it so happened that Montgomery was a tremendous disciplinarian, which was what was needed. He was also a dedicated, believing Christian. In about two months he revolutionized that army and changed its character and the activity of its officers, restored confidence and discipline, and then fought and won the first major Allied victory of the war, which was the battle of El Alamein. About two days after the battle had been fought I was in the desert with a three-ton truck, listening to a little portable radio in the back of the truck. A news commentator was describing over the radio the scene at Montgomery's headquarters the night before the battle at El Alamein was fought. He described how Montgomery called together his officers and men and publicly said, "Let us ask the Lord, mighty in battle, to give us the victory." In other words, he made a public statement of his faith in God and his dependence on God.

When that announcement came over the radio God spoke very quietly to my spirit and said, "This is the answer to your prayer." It was exactly what I had prayed for. Well, I think that was an initial experience in my life that had a deep effect, so when I became deeply concerned about the destiny of the United States, I can say that for about eight years I have prayed consistently, "Raise up the righteous and put down the wicked." And I haven't prayed it with any specific idea of who was righteous or who was wicked, or that it ought to be a Republican or that it ought to be a Democrat.

I also wrote a book entitled *Shaping History Through Prayer and Fasting*, which contains this kind of message in detailed form. Just after I had sent the book to the publishers the Watergate scandal broke upon the nation, and has continued up to the climax in the last few days. I trust this does not seem arrogant, but had I known everything that was going to happen in the next year and a half, I wouldn't have changed one word of what I had written in that book. I have a friend who is a committed Catholic Christian and leader of a Catholic group in a university city, and I had shared with him over a period of time my particular prayers for the government of the United States. So when the Watergate scandal broke he said to me one day, "Brother Prince, I hold you responsible for what is going on in Washington, D.C."

I said, "I gladly accept the responsibility."

ANTHONY: There is a prayer that Montgomery gave in the desert in 1941, and today the new president, Gerald Ford, gave a similar prayer. He said he recognizes that he was not voted into office, and so he asked that rather than a vote or a ballot, that tonight we confirm his new office with a prayer.

PRINCE: I respect that statement of his desire.

ANTHONY: He also asked that we pray that the peace President Nixon had worked for in the world, now be placed on his shoulders, the peace from above that passes all understanding.

Derek, there is a Scripture which says, "Ye are the salt of the earth: but if the salt has lost its savour, wherewith shall it be salted? It is thenceforth good for nothing, but to be cast out, and to be trodden under foot of men" (Matthew 5:13). Recently I was in a meeting with some people who are in positions of authority in Texas politics. We had been involved in politics for years, and no one ever thought about asking the question, "Well, what will the Christians think of this?" I wonder if maybe some of us have lost our savour and are being trodden under foot of men?

PRINCE: You have quoted one of my favorite Scriptures. First of all, I don't believe Christians play their cards right. In the last century Charles Finney, who was a man of

God and a great evangelist, made a statement to the effect
that Christians should agree on certain basic political principles: namely, that they would not vote for a man who was
a known reprobate in morals or ethics or other aspects of
his character; that they would only vote for men of proven
moral worth and integrity. Finney implied that there are
enough Christians in the United States, if we take Christians of all denominational backgrounds who all accept a
basic standard of morality, that if they really agree on that,
it would influence the political parties. They would be
under pressure to put up candidates of a character that
would meet those requirements.

It is obvious that if that one thing alone were done it
would change the whole character and tone of politics. I
still believe it is a practical possibility. I believe I have no
right as a Christian to cast my vote for a known reprobate,
no matter how attractive his policies may be. I believe God
has shown me from the Bible that if we vote for unworthy
leaders, morally, ethically, unworthy men, God will use
those same leaders to judge us. And I think this has happened in various instances in political history.

I also believe that one of the great functions of salt—
and there are many—is that salt restrains corruption. Before the time of refrigeration, when people wanted to pre-
serve meat on long sea voyages, they would use salt. The
meat was essentially corruptible, but the salt restrained the
corruption in that meat for weeks or months. I believe this
is a parable about our position as Christians. I believe there
is corruption at work in the world in human nature, in
society. But while we are here on the earth one of our
primary responsiblities is to restrain that corruption,
whether it is political, moral or social. If we fail to do that,
then we become salt that has lost its savour; we are not
doing our job. And Jesus said, "It is thenceforth good for
nothing." That's total condemnation, really.

ANTHONY: "To be trodden under foot of men."

PRINCE: Yes, and I believe it will be men's feet that will tread us under, I think history proves this. Saltless, apostate Christianity has usually gone under the feet of conquering barbarians or Muhammadans or Communists, and I think it is a definite, specific judgment of God. I think the destiny of American Christians hangs in the balance now, as to whether we will exercise our influence in restraining corruption and being the means of bringing back a demand for honesty and integrity, or whether we'll let things slide and perish.

ANTHONY: Don't you believe the Lord is coming soon?

PRINCE: I believe the Lord's coming is imminent, but just how imminent, I don't believe anybody really knows.

ANTHONY: The Scriptures tell us of certain things which must come to pass before the return of the Lord, and if we are praying that those things don't come to pass, then aren't we praying that the Lord will delay His coming? Am I seeing things wrong there?

PRINCE: The disciples asked Jesus, "What will be the sign of Thy coming, and of the end of the world?" (Matthew 24:3). The words are specific—"the sign.". In the rest of the chapter Jesus gives a number of signs like war, famines, pestilences, earthquakes, abounding lawlessness, false prophets, and so forth. But He hasn't actually answered the question until verse 14. There He says, "And this gospel of the kingdom shall be preached in all the world for a witness unto all nations; and then shall the end come." I deduce from that that the initiative is with the Church. It is not the business of the politicians or the military commanders to preach the gospel. The decisive factor in precipitating the end of the age is not the force of evil, but the activity of the Church.

ANTHONY: That is fascinating.

PRINCE: I think we Christians fail to understand how significant we are. We act as though we're a little insignificant minority that can just barely hold out until Jesus comes. I've come to view the Church at the close of the age in a totally different way. I believe it is an exceeding great army, and it is going to storm the gates of Hades and triumphantly proclaim Christ to every nation on earth. After that, let the end come.

ANTHONY: I've never heard it taught that way, Derek. That is a brilliant insight. It is the Christians who control it, not the demonic forces of evil.

PRINCE: Absolutely. You said it as clearly as it could be said. You see, we are the Body of Christ, and God will always use the Body of Christ to effect His main purposes in the earth. He will not bypass us. So the initiative is with us because it is with Christ.

Another Scripture I like is in Psalm 110. God said to Christ, "Thou art a priest forever after the order of Melchizedek." He also said, "Rule Thou in the midst of Thine enemies." I see that most Christians are more taken up with the enemies than they are with Christ. But the Scripture indicates to me that Christ is already now ruling.

ANTHONY: It seems to me we are always so sin-conscious we forget to be Son-conscious.

PRINCE: I agree. I may be a little controversial here, but I think the basic idea of the average church-going Christian is that if you are holy you ought to feel guilty, and if you don't feel guilty there is something wrong with you. In fact, I think many of our hymns and many of our church activities and liturgies are designed almost to make you feel guilty.

ANTHONY: They make you feel rotten.

PRINCE: I think this is totally out of line with the purpose of God. Scripture says, "God was in Christ, reconciling the world unto Himself, not imputing their trespas-

ses unto them" (2 Corinthians 5:19). I don't think God
wants us to feel guilty. God's aim is to make us feel righteous in Christ, because without Christ there is no righteousness. But I'm afraid we've stopped at this conscious-
ness of sin level and we talk and think of ourselves in a
belittling way, "I'm just a poor sinner saved by grace." My
comment on that is, if that is all grace has done for you, you
had very little grace.

This is a very critical issue. When I preach I take people
to the plain statements and promises of the Bible; I don't
offer them my opinions. I show people the clear promises
in the Bible. Let's take 2 Chronicles 7:14: "If My people,
which are called by My name, shall humble themselves,
and pray, and seek My face, and turn from their wicked
ways; then will I hear from heaven, and will forgive their
sin, and will heal their land." I argue that the healing of our
land depends upon the people of God in the land. People's
attitude is, "Oh, that's impossible. Evil is getting worse
and worse; tribulation is coming; the Antichrist is coming." I say, "Well, God didn't command me to wait for the
Antichrist. He told me to wait for the Christ. My eyes are
on Christ, not on Antichrist."

Then I ask people this question: "Do you believe the
power of evil in the world will ever be so great that God will
no longer be able to keep His promises?"

The average Christian will never answer, "Yes."

Then I say, "All we're talking about are the promises of
God. Let's meet His conditions and leave it to Him to fulfill
them."

ANTHONY: Somebody once said that the greatest
way to doubt God is to fear Satan.

PRINCE: I think there is a way we can recognize how
real, how malicious, how cunning Satan is. I think we need
to do that. But having done that, we need to know that he is

a defeated enemy, and that the weapons belong to us, not to Satan.

ANTHONY: The Bible says: "Now the Spirit speaketh expressly, that in the latter times some shall depart from the faith, giving heed to seducing spirits and doctrines of devils; Speaking lies in hypocrisy; having their conscience seared with a hot iron" (1 Timothy 4:1, 2). It is obviously talking about Christians because it says they will depart from the faith. Is that right, Derek?

PRINCE: I believe that is the obvious way to interpret it. My experience is amply borne out in what I see happening to people. We were talking about Christians being the salt of the earth and having decisive influence which cannot be exercised by any other group. I think the basic principle of this is that the decisive factors in human affairs are spiritual factors. Obviously spiritual factors cause things to happen and take place. Whoever takes mastery in the spiritual realm will see that mastery work out in history, for example in social events, and in military events.

This is another reason why the Church is the salt of the earth. The Church is the only group on earth that has the effect it needs to intervene in the spiritual realm. Paul says in Ephesians 6:12 that our wrestling match is "not against flesh and blood, but against principalities, against powers, against the rulers of the darkness of this world, against spiritual wickedness in high places." That can sound rather melodramatic, but I believe it means we are in conflict with the spiritual forces which seek to dominate and destroy the human race. That conflict is one of our major assignments as Christians.

My comment is that too many Christians put the period in the wrong place in this passage. They say, "We wrestle not," period. That's the end of it. But that is not the way it is written. Again, Paul says, "The weapons of our warfare are not carnal, but mighty through God to the pulling down of strongholds; Casting down imaginations, and every high thing that exalteth itself against the knowledge of God" (2 Corinthians 10:4, 5). Paul says we are in a spiritual warfare. We have the spiritual weapons, and they are adequate to the task. They will cast down everything that opposes the true knowledge of God, everything that takes men's imaginations or thoughts into captivity. We can liberate men's imaginations and thoughts. We can cast down Satan's strongholds. We alone have the spiritual weapon. The world has what Paul calls carnal weapons: bombs, guns, planes, tanks, which are effective in their area, but they are totally ineffective in the spiritual realm. The only group qualified to intervene in the spiritual realm is the Church of Jesus Christ. That's why we are the salt of the earth. We have the ability to change things in the spiritual realm in God's favor and for the fulfillment of God's purpose. If we fail to do that, then we are salt that's lost its savour.

ANTHONY: Is that part of the whole process of intercession?

PRINCE: Well, intercession is one major means to do that. But I think intercession has got to be based on a pretty clear understanding of spiritual realities. You know, intercession is not, "God bless America." But intercession has got to get down to the nitty-gritty of what is wrong with America and how to deal with it. Here I will venture an opinion. My personal conviction is that in America, Public Enemy Number One is witchcraft. There are two forms of witchcraft: there is the open form of witchcraft which is the deliberate cultivation of Satan and his power which is rampant in this nation today in many different forms—but they are all basically an acknowledgment of Satan and an attempt to cultivate and utilize his power. But more subtle and dangerous, in a way, is what I call undisclosed witchcraft. Here I am going to say something which to some will be very controversial. But the essence of witchcraft is that it enables the female to dominate the male, which is contrary to divine order. If you go back to the origin of the human race as revealed in Scripture, all trouble began when Eve became the counselor and Adam accepted her advice. Though that may seem simple, it contains the root of all our problems. It was the reverse of divine order in which the man is the head of the woman. Essentially, Satan has always attacked the human race this way.

ANTHONY: How about also through seeking your own?

PRINCE: The motivation introduced by Satan was, "Ye shall be as gods." In other words, "You won't need to depend upon God." He didn't tempt them into drunkenness or immorality or theft. Again, I think the basic motivation of sin is the desire to be independent of God, and many times people use things that are apparently good. Many religious people use their religion to make themselves independent from God. They want to be so good, so religious, that they don't need God. So there is an unseen force at work. It is a deceptive force. It plays upon man's personal ambition and his desire to exalt himself. But it's very cunning, and it is particularly manifest, in my personal opinion, in the United States, which is essentially a woman-dominated society as is no other society that I am familiar with anywhere. I think as a result of this the whole social structure is out of line with God's purpose. I predict that the greatest revolution that's ever going to take place in America is at the door. It is the restoration of order in the home with the man taking back the responsibilities of his home, the priest and prophet in his house; restoration of male leadership in the church; and restoration of God's authority in the nation. This, I believe, is the spiritual battle we are fighting, and it is a tremendous conflict.

ANTHONY: What does that passage in Timothy mean, "In the latter times some shall depart from the faith, giving heed to seducing spirits and doctrines of devils."?

PRINCE: Well, Satan is the archdeceiver. He operates primarily by deception.

ANTHONY: Can he operate in the name of Christ?

PRINCE: He can operate in the name of religion and he can present himself as representing Christ. Paul says about certain people that they "are false apostles, deceitful workers, transforming themselves into the apostles of Christ" (2 Corinthians 11:13). Then he said, "And no marvel; for Satan himself is transformed into an angel of light" (verse 14). I think Satan's greatest deceptions are religious deceptions, and he is not by any means beneath presenting deceptions under Christian headings and titles. In fact, as I view the Scripture, at the end of the age there are going to be only two religious groups. In the Bible one is categorized as the Bride; the other is categorized as the Harlot. If we ask ourselves what will be the difference, I think when viewed in those terms the answer is very simple. The Bride has remained faithful to her commitment to Jesus Christ. The Harlot has denied Him.

ANTHONY: Someone has said there are two ways you can tell whether you are in Christ. One is that your eyes are never on yourself; and the second is that you will always reflect the fruit of the Spirit.

PRINCE: I agree with that, but I would like to put it this way. The center of Christianity is Christ. What we are confronted with in many churches today is a Christless Christianity or a religion that eliminates Jesus Christ. A friend of mine in a well-known major denominational church said to me the other day, "In our church you can talk about anybody you like; you can talk about Socrates, Buddha, Plato, Martin Luther King, and there's no trouble.

But if you talk about Jesus everybody gets upset." This is a very obvious trend taking place in Christendom, to eliminate that awkward historical figure, Jesus of Nazareth. The idea is, "Get Him out of the way, and we can all unite." We can all believe in God in some way; the stumbling block is Jesus Christ.

I see this process far advanced. Essentially, no matter how Satan may operate in details, his aim is to alienate a person from total commitment to Jesus Christ. And he always ultimately works to dishonor Jesus Christ. You see it in the denial of the virgin birth. It leaves only one conclusion: Jesus was a bastard. And there are only two possible explanations of His birth. Well, that is totally dishonoring to Jesus Christ. Ultimately, Satan has a further objective. He wants to eliminate Jesus Christ and then take the place of Jesus Christ. That is the true meaning of Antichrist. Satan is at work eliminating Jesus Christ in order to take His place.

ANTHONY: I am sure there are some people saying, "Okay, I agree there are some seducing spirits and doctrines of demons going around—maybe even in what I am listening to in some teachings. What do I do? How do I know? How do I protect myself?"

PRINCE: That is a good question. I think one helpful statement is that which Jesus said: "I am the way, the truth, and the life" (John 14:6). If you really know the truth about Jesus you will not be deceived. I've found that all people who go into error are people who do not know the basic teaching about Jesus, His eternal nature, His deity, His virgin birth, His sinless life, His substitutionary atonement, His physical death, His physical resurrection, His ascension into heaven, and the fact that He is coming again physically in the same way in which He went. If you hold fast to those facts I do not believe you will go into error. They are not new; all the great confessions of faith of the

Christian church have always asserted those as the central facts of the Christian faith. But I think we can make it more simple for people by saying, "Accept Jesus totally as He is presented in the Bible." You may have your problems, you may have your doubts, but you'll come through.

But if you turn away from Jesus . . . . You see, the very word "seducing" actually has a sexual connotation. What a seducing spirit does is to seduce somebody who should be the Bride to become part of the Harlot. In other words, everything ultimately depends upon our total loyalty to Jesus Christ.

ANTHONY: There are other people who are being more directly affected than just on the basis of the teachings. They're hearing voices and being directly affected by these things, and it seems to be happening a great deal.

PRINCE: Paul says there are so many kinds of voices in the world. One of the most important things to know is, "Is the voice speaking to me the voice of God?" I deal every week with people who hear voices that tell them to do strange things, and sometimes they are very religious things, like give all their money to the poor. I say you've got to be very sure the voice you hear is the voice of God. Let me say from experience, if people have in any way at any time been involved in the occult, they are exposed to deception. Even when they become Christians or confess faith in Jesus Christ, they are liable still to have the occult, deceiving influences at work in their lives. It really demands a deliberate, total renunciation of every involvement with the occult, and a willingness to part with every association—burn every book, get rid of every image, idol or charm.

I've dealt with people who have worshipped Satan. I've discovered that they almost always have to burn every article of clothing they ever used in any context of Satanic worship. There has to be a total break with every area of the occult. Jesus said, "I am the way, the truth, and the life: no man cometh unto the Father but by me." There are many ways into the supernatural world, but there is only one way that leads to Light and Truth and God the Father, and that is by Jesus Christ. I know this by experience, because before I came to know the Lord Jesus I experimented with many of these things. I was into practicing yoga, and I got into the supernatural realm. But I got into darkness, misery, fear and bondage, not into the realm of Light and Truth and love and freedom.

ANTHONY: Isn't it ironic that in order to be totally free you have to be totally bound? It's a paradox.

PRINCE: Yes, it is. But it's one the human heart understands, really.

ANTHONY: What about people who are hearing voices? People who say, "Well, God talks to people. He talked to all those people in the Bible, and God is talking to me. He told me to do this or to do that." What about that?

PRINCE: The highest level of divine revelation is in the Scriptures, and the Scriptures themselves clearly claim that the Holy Spirit is the author of Scripture. The Holy Spirit is consistent; He doesn't deny Himself nor contradict Himself. So anything that will be said to us personally, directly by the Holy Spirit will be in line with Scripture. If it is not in line with Scripture it is not the Holy Spirit. Then again, the Holy Spirit uplifts and glorifies Jesus. Consequently, any revelation from the Holy Spirit will glorify the Lord Jesus Christ. Again, the Holy Spirit is a Spirit of truth. If He predicts anything it will come to pass. If you receive predictions which are only partially fulfilled, this must mean that it did not come entirely from the Holy Spirit.

ANTHONY: I'm going to put you on the spot now. I've been in prayer meetings where unconditional prophecies were given. I understand conditional prophecy—"if this comes true then that will happen." But there were unconditional prophecies saying that such and such is going to happen, and it didn't come true. And this was in prayer meetings in the name of Jesus.

PRINCE: Well, you see, the fact that people use the name of Jesus is no guarantee they are right. In fact, if they knew the Scripture, they would not make the error, because the Bible says, "Despise not prophesying. Prove all things; hold fast that which is good" (1 Thessalonians 5:20, 21). All prophecy given in the New Testament is to be checked. People who will not submit their prophecy to testing are wrong in their spiritual attitude to start with. "Let the prophets speak two or three, and let the other judge" (1 Corinthians 14:29). There is no such thing as absolute authority in prophecy in the New Testament church.

ANTHONY: Another favorite Scripture is, "Study to show thyself approved unto God, a workman that needeth not to be ashamed, rightly dividing the word of truth" (2 Timothy 2:15).

PRINCE: It takes study and application to become acquainted with the Scripture. One test of the Holy Spirit's activity is He always creates a hunger for the Word of God. So if it is the Spirit of God at work, He will cause you to take more time with your Bible, to be more interested in the Scripture. If it is keeping you away from the Bible, then it is not the Spirit of God.

Another thing about the Holy Spirit is, He will always give us love for Jesus Christ and love for our fellow Christians. If these forces are not at work, then the kind of revelational voice the person is hearing is not from God.

One of the things the devil likes to do to deceive people is to isolate them, get them away by themselves. Somehow they are the only ones who have the truth. They are more spiritual; others don't see it. But once the devil has you isolated, he will destroy you bit by bit. There's a certain safety in belonging to a fellowship of believers, even if they do silly things and make mistakes. If you remain in the fellowship you remain in the light.

ANTHONY: We're into some strong meat here, because there are many people who are being deceived aren't there?

PRINCE: Yes, many. But the Bible says in the latter times many shall depart from the faith and there will be many false prophets, and they shall deceive many. We've been warned. We don't need to be deceived if our attitude toward God is right.

ANTHONY: A lot of people are spending all their time judging others.

PRINCE: There is another statement about prophecy. "But he that prophesieth speaketh unto men to edification, and exhortation, and comfort" (1 Corinthians 14:3). There's no room for condemnation in New Testament prophecy. I've heard prophesying that has left people confused, condemned and frustrated. Well, that is not the activity of the fruit of the Spirit in the believer's life. I know such prophesying is not from God.

ANTHONY: Is the fruit of the Spirit the personality of Christ?

PRINCE: I suppose one could say that. In a way it is the Christ nature being manifest in the person.

ANTHONY: What about dying? Paul talks a lot about dying; do you think we talk about it enough?

PRINCE: Many groups don't. The Bible speaks about the "old man" which is our nature inherited from Adam, and the Bible presents the old man very crudely as a criminal. He is a criminal. There is a criminal inside every one of us, and his activity will betray his nature. God has only one remedy for the old man. He doesn't send him to church; He doesn't teach him Scripture; He executes him. The execution took place in Christ on the cross; our old man was crucified with Him. We've got to make that effective in our experience by a decision of our will.

ANTHONY: Two words seem to be critical: "reckon" and "let."

PRINCE: Yes, and "crucified." "They that are Christ's have crucified the flesh with the affections and lusts" (Galatians 5:24).

LAWRENCE LADIGBOLU

Lawrence Ladigbolu has one of the most outstanding stories in Christendom today. He was a member of the royal family of a Nigerian tribe of sixteen million people, a prince, an Islamic evangelist, soon to be king of his particular tribe, a controller of immense wealth. He then lost everything and his family disowned him because he said, "Jesus is my life." He was banned from his country. When I first met him he was trimming hedges on the Southern Methodist University campus in Dallas, and living in one small room while he was studying and learning more about this Christ who had come into his life.

CHAPTER 7

LAWRENCE LADIGBOLU

If you accept this Jesus you are no longer my son
. . . you must leave our country.

ANTHONY: Our guest tonight is Lawrence Ladigbolu. I can't pronounce his last name, so I'll just call him Brother Lawrence. He is from Nigeria. It is possible that he still could become the king of sixteen million people in Nigeria. He is a past Muslim evangelist, and was excommunicated by his people and his country. He is in the United States going to seminary. We're going to talk tonight about choices. Just imagine if you had the opportunity to become a king of sixteen million people, what would go through your heart?

Lawrence, how did you come to know the Lord? Tell us about your background and that moment when you first believed.

LAWRENCE: It all happened twelve years ago, and twelve years ago to me now looks just like a year ago because of the joy I found in coming to Jesus and trusting Him. I was born and brought up in an entirely Muslim home. In addition to being a Muslim home, it was also a rare family. My grandfather was king, and my father had the potential of becoming king. Everything was laid out before me, and I felt I was doing very well. I was sent to an Arabic school where I learned to read and write the Arabic figures and to recite the Koran, and I loved doing that so much. I had many friends among the Muslims, especially among the ones who go about preaching Islam.

In the years when I was going to the Arabic school I became an interpreter. I became so good at it that I became an evangelist's assistant, so everywhere he went I went with him.

ANTHONY: And he was a Muslim evangelist?

LAWRENCE: Yes, and I too became an evangelist. All along I was doing this because I felt it was something I could do to gain some favor from God, so my balance of merits would outweigh the balance of demerits on the day of judgment.

ANTHONY: So you could work your way into heaven?

LADIGBOLU: Yes, that's what you could call it. As a matter of fact, I was a real Muslim in my own understanding of being a Muslim, and very religious. This continued for six or seven years. That was from 1952 to 1959.

Then I went to a secondary modern school, and there for the first time I met a group of Christian people who, having known me from my touring and preaching Islam about the place, started talking to me about the Bible. They did not talk to me about the Lord Jesus, but about the Bible. They were Jehovah's Witnesses. This preacher liked to read the Bible, and compare notes with what I was preaching in Islam and what he was preaching in the Bible, and see where we agree and where we disagree. That is how I was introduced to the Bible. In fact, they gave me the first Bible I ever had.

Because I found some of the stories in the Bible the same as the stories in the Koran, I started reading the Bible. I started in the Old Testament and read the stories of Abraham, Isaac, and Joseph. I found them very interesting. They were interesting because I could read them in my own native language, which I could not do in the Koran. I had to read the Koran in Arabic, then translate it to my native language. Gradually I became more and more interested in talking about what is in the Bible and asking questions from these people. While I appreciate what they did for me, they still didn't do enough. They didn't show me the truth; they didn't show me the way that could satisfy the longings of my heart.

After my years in the secondary modern school, I took a teaching appointment. In 1961 I met my first Christian brother and friend, who, seeing I was interested in reading the Bible, and knowing and hearing of my past experiences as a Muslim evangelist, came to me and said, "Ayo (which is my native name), I know you are religious, but you need just one thing."

I said, "What do I need? I need nothing, because I already believe. There is one God, and I believe in Him, and Muhammad is His prophet. I need nothing more."

This friend patiently said, "Ayo, you do need something. I know you are very zealous, you are very religious. But you need the peace and joy that Jesus can give you."

I said, "Well, I don't know . . . I don't know."

He said, "You don't know what?"

I said, "Well, I don't know about that. I know about Jesus. I know He was born by Mary; I know His father was Joseph; I know everything about Him. But how do you know He was one of the prophets, after Muhammad came to fulfill all prophecies? You talk like this, but I don't know."

ANTHONY: But you knew all about Him?

LADIGBOLU: Yes, I knew all about Him, but I didn't know Him for myself. This friend helped me, and I am sure he, with many others, must have been praying for me. In these discussions he would say, "You turn to the New Testament and read the Gospel of John. You just read it, and if you have questions, I'll come back and we can talk about it."

Gradually I felt the Spirit of God was dealing with me face to face with the reality of my life as a person, rather than my life as a Muslim evangelist, or as a school teacher or as a religious person. I started thinking. If the Bible says that God loved the world and He sent Jesus, that those who believe in Him might be saved, and as this friend continues to say, this might not exclude me, but it should include me. If I go back home and say I have become a Christian, I will lose all the respect among the people that I have already established with my position as a Muslim evangelist. All my friends would run away from me. Well, what other possibilities are there? My father didn't go to school. I did go to school, and I have some education. I studied the prospects of maybe becoming a king when it comes to the time of my line in the family. And everybody at home are Muslims. No, I won't, I won't.

ANTHONY: That was too much to give up?

LADIGBOLU: For all these things, I just didn't think I could. But this friend persisted, and all along I read the Bible. And then it happened one day. Throughout the year 1961 I didn't give up my Islam, I didn't give up all these big things I had been considering, because I dared not. But in 1962, I came back after the Christmas holiday to resume teaching in the school. This friend came back to me and said, "Well, now that you're back, I think you've had enough time to consider it. God loves you. He wants to save you and He wants to use you. Now you can't run away from Him."

I told him, "Okay, I'll give it a try." In my ignorance I said, "What can I do that this faith, this hope, this life you have been talking about can become mine?"

He said, "Come on." We went into his room and sat down and he said, "Repeat the sinner's prayer after me."

I said, "What prayer?"

"Lord Jesus, I've been running away from you a long time, but today I want to give up everything and give myself to You, to do with my life what You will." As I said that prayer, it was so wonderful, brother! The tears were falling down my face and the heavy load was just going down, and I felt a peace I had never known come into my heart. And that was it!

ANTHONY: That's pretty neat. In Nigeria, in this decision process you went through, deciding you didn't want to give up the respect of the people and being a Muslim evangelist, the potential of being a king of sixteen million people, you finally gave those things all up for Jesus. Now a king in Nigeria is absolute ruler, isn't he?

LADIGBOLU: Yes, he is, in the sense that the people regard him as second only to God, and his word is final on many issues. But now with the British type of administration and democracy, the king doesn't have the last word on everything. But still, he is venerated and respected by his people.

ANTHONY: Did you consciously know at the moment Christ came into your heart, when you said that simple prayer—did you know you were giving all that up? Did you really understand what you were saying when you said the prayer, "Jesus, I give You my everything"?

LADIGBOLU: No, I didn't fully at that moment. I didn't fully consider the implications which were to come afterwards, though all along I had been thinking of all these things. They were things which made it difficult for me, and made it slower for me to really decide for Christ. But at that moment I just forgot about everything.

ANTHONY: Like the butterfly. It crawls out of its cocoon and flies away, and it forgets all the past.

LADIGBOLU: I just forgot about those things. But they came back smack in my face later.

ANTHONY: What happened with your family, your grandfather and your parents? What happened when you went back and told them that you were a Christian?

LADIGBOLU: Well, I didn't go back immediately, because after this, I started going to church in the little village where I was teaching school.

ANTHONY: That must have caused a stir in that little village.

LADIGBOLU: Many people couldn't believe it. They thought I was going to church because I was a school teacher, but because I had not been going for one year since I had come to that village, some of them were asking me. Some of them called me "Prince," some of them called me by my first name.

ANTHONY: "Prince" was a title you deserved because of your family. But now you are the child of another King!

LADIGBOLU: Yes, I sure am. The people would say, "Prince, what's happened? You're going to church!"

"Well, I'm going to church." Because they respected me, some of them would not ask any more questions. They would say, "Are you going to church?" I would answer, "Yes, I'm going to church," and that's all.

But some bolder ones would say, "We are surprised; you are going to church. Why?"

I would say, "I am going to church because I have become a follower of Jesus." But I couldn't go home right away. It took me four months after January, 1962, before I could go home and make this known.

ANTHONY: What was the first thing that happened? Who were you closest to in your entire family back home?

LADIGBOLU: My father.

ANTHONY: What was the first thing that happened when you told him? How did it happen?

LADIGBOLU: Well, I didn't tell him directly. I would do something and wait for him to react. One day when I was there for the weekend, after showering and shaving, I said, "I'll see you," and I went out. He didn't question me where I was going. But several people saw me go into the church, and it caused quite a stir. Then before I went back home to tell my father and my mother and my brother and my friends, the people said, "We don't know what has happened, but we saw him in church."

My father said, "He might have gone with some of his friends. Maybe they had some big 'do' at the church and he just accompanied his friends there. Otherwise, it couldn't be." So he just dismissed it as nothing, but said he would ask me when I returned.

So when I got back the first thing he did was to say, "Welcome. Why church? Why did you go to it?"

I said, "Church?"

He said, "Now, don't deny it, because about five people saw you and have come here to tell me. What are you going to do? I even defended you. I said it was not serious, but you had just gone with some friends."

I said, "No, I'm not going with friends. I went on my own. I have been going to church for four months before today back in my station."

He just couldn't take it. He said, "Church? Four months? What?"

I knew he could become very, very furious and anything could happen that night, so I just walked out.

ANTHONY: Was he a violent man?

LADIGBOLU: He wasn't violent in the sense of doing anything harmful to me, but by the look on his face I knew that he had received the shock of his life.

ANTHONY: What did you feel at that moment when you were confronted by your father? That instant when he knew you had become a follower of Jesus, what did you feel for him at that moment? Was it fear as to how he would react?

LADIGBOLU: That was a big part of my feelings, because at that moment he said, "You? You—went to church?" I felt very bad and afraid and I didn't know what would result from it, but I went out quietly, went to my own apartment and waited there. About half an hour later he sent for me, and before that he had gotten all the old people (elders) out in the compound together and they were all sitting there waiting for me.

He said, "Son, repeat what you told me half an hour ago before these people who are mothers and fathers and to whom we all belong. Tell them what you just told me."

I said, in all humility, "Fathers and mothers, I have told my father when I came back from church what happened to me, and that is, I am a Christian. I am following Jesus. That is because when I said to Him, 'Yes, come in,' I felt much different than I have ever felt in all my life. And I know something has happened to me, and that is why I am a Christian. I didn't want to be forced to tell my father, but some people saw me in church and reported to him and I couldn't deny it, because no matter how long I kept it, I was still going to tell him. So that is my story."

ANTHONY: You made an interesting statement there; you said, "Fathers and mothers." Does that mean the elders?

LADIGBOLU: It was all the people who were gathered around. It was considered a family meeting. There were uncles and sisters and aunts and other people who were related to me.

ANTHONY: Then they were part of the royal family?

LADIGBOLU: Yes, they were a part of the royal family.

ANTHONY: So in our understanding of, say, the king of England, this is analogous to his son becoming something totally and completely opposed to their whole way of life, isn't it?

LADIGBOLU: Yes.

ANTHONY: Later, I want to ask you about how one can talk to the Black Muslims. This is a popular movement in the United States now. But those of us in the United States can't really understand all that you gave up to be a Christian—the respect of your family, possibly being heir to a throne and having control over sixteen million people. When you ask someone here whether they are a Christian they say, "Well, of course I am. I'm an American, aren't I?" They don't understand what it means to be born again or what it means to be a follower of Jesus. The contrast is so great in your life. I envy you that experience.

What were some of the later results in your family? Did your father try to convert you back to Islam?

LADIGBOLU: He did everything to bring me back to Islam. The family was so organized. My uncle, who was then king, was one of those designated to talk to me and to bring me back. Then all his friends, and all my friends—the ones I had known since childhood and whom I loved very much—they all started backing out and not having anything to do with me. Then my father called me in and said, "Now, son, you have decided you are not coming back?" This is how he put it: "Naked fire and gunpowder cannot live together in the same house. You and I cannot stay under the same roof. You know our position; you know your position; you know everything about this family and what shame you are now bringing on us. So, until you decide to come back, you are excused. You must live outside this place."

ANTHONY: So where did you live?

LADIGBOLU: Well, I went to my mother's side. They are not Christians, but since my father had thrown me out, they could not throw me out. I stayed with them some of the time; some of the time I stayed with Christian brothers and friends. And I still had my job as a schoolteacher, so I could still take proper care of myself.

ANTHONY: What about your students? Did parents of the students rebel against your being their teacher?

LADIGBOLU: No, nothing like that happened. The government pays all the teachers' salaries, and the parents have very little control about what goes on in the school. Having their children taught was their only concern. The Lord showed me I could work harder than I had before. When I became a Christian I didn't like some things that I used to like, like going out with my friends and boozing and all these things we enjoyed as young people. The Lord helped me to live by the power of the Spirit so the people could say, "We like this teacher."

ANTHONY: What does it mean if I say "sonship" to you?

LADIGBOLU: Sonship, to me, really took a different turn of meaning at the time I came to the Lord in 1962.

ANTHONY: You were already the son of a king.

LADIGBOLU: Yes, I was the son of a king, but it seems the king had said to me, "You are no longer my son." But I have the peace that I am a son of God, who is the King of kings. That's what I would tell my friends who would come and say, "Look, you have thrown everything away. Look at you!" I would say, "Well, I am glad, because now I am the son of the King of kings." What more could anybody ask?

ANTHONY: I notice you have the scars of tribal markings along your cheeks. What do they mean?

LADIGBOLU: In my own part of Nigeria, the northern part, the different tribes have marks. These marks may belong to the family, a large household, or to a tribal group. There are lots of stories about when they started putting these marks on people, and how it was done, and the reasons for doing it. But the particular marks which I have on my face are the marks of the royal family, of the Yoruba kingdom, the Alafin of the Oyo royal family.

ANTHONY: So only the royal family has those unique scars on their face?

LADIGBOLU: Yes, these are family scars, and these are the marks of the royal household to which I belong. All our tribes and families have marks, but these particular marks are of the royal household.

ANTHONY: You are attending seminary here in Dallas?

LADIGBOLU: Yes.

ANTHONY: It must be kind of strong to have been an Islam evangelist, and all of a sudden, now you are a minister of Christ. That's neat, isn't it?

LADIGBOLU: When I became a Christian, after the three years of exile . . .

ANTHONY: What does that mean?

LADIGBOLU: Well, I was sent away from home and my father had nothing to do with me. Then he softened up and called me back. Do you know what he said? He said, "Ayo, I will absolve you. I feel that this new faith of yours is good for you. We would like to belong to the same thing with you, but we can't, because . . . " And then he listed all the reasons I knew why he could not.

ANTHONY: What about members of your family?

LADIGBOLU: Just one brother has come to the Lord.

ANTHONY: Wouldn't it be a miracle if your father came to the Lord? Is he still living?

LADIGBOLU: No, he passed away last year. But one of my brothers came to the Lord. He lived with us for two years, after I had gone to Bible school and become a Christian evangelist in Nigeria. He stayed with us and we prayed for him and talked to him about the Lord, and he decided for Jesus.

ANTHONY: The markings on your face are readily recognizable by most of the tribes in Nigeria, right? I mean, that's your badge, so to speak. That's your identification as part of the royal family. Now, what did people think about a member of the royal family from the house of Islam coming and talking about Jesus?

LADIGBOLU: Well, some of them felt surprised. Some people thought it was incredible.

ANTHONY: Did they recognize you immediately from your face markings?

LADIGBOLU: Oh, yes. Some just said, "Things are changing, and this is one of the changes we are going through."

ANTHONY: Do you see the fruit of the Christian labor in Africa?

LADIGBOLU: Yes, and for that I really praise God because my desire, like Paul's, is to talk about Jesus. I am not ashamed to talk about Him and to repeat the gospel, because I believe it is the power of God unto salvation for everyone who believes. For me, for the Jews, for everybody in Africa, in Europe, even here in America—for everybody who believes. So I am delighted to say that our people are reaching out now, even to the Muslims in the north of Nigeria, and others report from the Nigeria Baptist city crusades that two-thousand people have come to know the Lord Jesus through the evangelistic outreach of the churches in Nigeria.

ANTHONY: You just came from Nigeria in September. For the last year or more we've heard tremendous things about the Spirit of God moving throughout most of Africa. It must be exciting to see. In fact, there is probably a greater spiritual revolution in Africa than there is here. We have missionaries right now in South Dallas who are from Africa. That's kind of neat, too.

You were saying it has been twelve years since you came to Christ, but it seems just like yesterday. That is beautiful. Before I came to the Lord I spent a lot of time studying the different religions, and I got into Islam and the Koran. Now all over the country we see a tremendous move toward the Black Muslim movement. As I see it, it is a prostitution of the original Muslim religion. It politicizes and mixes some Scripture in there, and makes it whatever they think is necessary to get the job done for the moment. A lot of people are asking about it. What do you say to the Black Muslims? How do you share with them? What do you think about the Muslims now?

LADIGBOLU: I think most people in Africa as well as in America, embrace Islam as a substitute. They are uninterested in Christianity. I have heard several people back home say that Islam is the religion of the black man, while Christianity, to them, is the white man's religion. And so, it is more a political identity. People are seeking political identity. You know, Islam, coming from Arabia, Egypt and North Africa—people just feel, "This comes from people who are like us, with the same color skin." So they are building their faith upon political ideologies, rather than on Scriptural truth. So to any man—black, white or whatever color—I would say that I have been a Muslim myself, and I did not find the peace and the joy and the hope which I now have. I did not find it when I was a Muslim; Christ is the answer to all men's needs.

ANTHONY: Shortly after I came to the Lord I went to a regional Black Muslim meeting, and I think I was the only white man in the meeting. It was a scary thing. I went through searches where I had to empty my pockets. It was a very organized and structured kind of situation. All the women sat on one side of the room in their habits. And I heard nothing but a message of hate. In fact, there was a lot of "kill whitey" kind of stuff. They were saying, "Kill that honky whitey" and looking at me, and I was getting nervous. But yet, when I remember what I read in the Koran, I don't remember that kind of a hate message in the Koran. How did it happen that they are calling themselves Black Muslims, and supposedly reading the Koran?

LADIGBOLU: From what I know of Islam—I have studied it and been in it myself—Muhammad acknowledged Jesus as the greatest of all the prophets, and he said people should listen to Him and obey Him. All through the life of the prophet Muhammad himself, in spite of the political battles he had to fight, and the religious battles he had to fight, he never preached hate. Through all my readings in the *Koran* and the *Hadith* and my dealings with Muslims in the places I have been, Islam is not meant to be a religion of hate. But as I said earlier, people embrace Islam as a substitute for Christianity, which they regard as the white man's religion. This is because Christianity has some racist nations representing it, such as South Africa, Rhodesia, Mozambique, Angola, and other places. So to many people today, Islam is something that belongs to the black man. But it is not a religion to them, it is a political system, though they may give it in the name of God.

ANTHONY: That is a shame. Someone asked, "How do you talk to a Black Muslim about the Lord?" Well, the same as you would talk to anybody. We are all human beings and we all have the same needs.

LADIGBOLU: Our needs are the same whether we live in slums and ghettos, or in Highland Park. Our basic problems are the same; we are all sinners. We are lost men, and without Christ we have no hope. In Him we find life, we find hope, we find meaning for life. We become whole; we become what God intends for us to be as human beings. We are able to listen to God, to obey Him, to do His will, and to live His life among other men and show love.

ANTHONY: Is your wife back in Nigeria?

LADIGBOLU: Yes.

ANTHONY: Are you going to try to bring her over here?

LADIGBOLU: I am planning to go back home in a year or a year and six months.

ANTHONY: Were you a Christian when you met her?

LADIGBOLU: No, she was a Muslim and I was a Muslim. But we both became Christians and got married.

ANTHONY: Who is Elijah Muhammad, and how is he related to Muhammad?

LADIGBOLU: Only when I came to this country did I hear about Elijah Muhammad. All I know about him is that he is the founder of the Black Muslim movement.

ANTHONY: He is not recognized in Islam?

LADIGBOLU: No, people hardly know about him in Nigeria. I didn't know about him until I came to the United States. I think his only relationship to Islam in general is that he is recognized here in this country as the founder of the Black Muslims.

ANTHONY: Share with us what the Lord is doing in your own life right now, Brother Lawrence.

LADIGBOLU: So many things—my heart is full. I could just keep on saying, "Praise the Lord." My life will be lived every day praising Him. Without faith in the Lord Jesus, without giving our whole life to Him, to take our controls off, it is difficult for one to find meaning for living, and to find hope for dying, and to find assurance for life that is eternal. So, if all our listeners will come to the Lord Jesus, give their lives to Him completely and make Him the master and Lord of their lives, then they will find life worth living. He has made it possible for me to find that it is worth living. The outflow of His Spirit in us, in anyone who comes to Him, will reach out to others and then people can see us and say, "Truly, he has been with the Lord."

COLONEL JIM IRWIN

Fighter pilot, jet jockey, test pilot, astronaut, one of twelve men in all of history who has ever walked on the moon—a man who found God while walking on that moon. Flying was his life and religion, but now he would give up flying in an instant to follow Christ. He has seen the earth from afar looking like a beautiful, fragile, delicate Christmas tree ornament hanging in the black timeless space. And the spiritual impact of seeing the earth from that perspective has irrevocably changed his life!

CHAPTER 8

COLONEL JIM IRWIN

I've trod the high untrespassed sanctity of space, put out my hand, and touched the face of God.

ANTHONY: The number twelve has a lot of significance. There were twelve men who followed Jesus, and there are twelve tribes of Israel. In today's world twelve has another meaning: there are twelve men who have walked on the moon. Can you imagine that only twelve men out of the millions of men who have ever lived have walked on the moon? Our guest tonight is one of them, Col. Jim Irwin. Jim, do you feel like you've been on the moon?

IRWIN: Sometimes I wonder, but if there is a moon in the sky then I look up there and it all becomes real again.

ANTHONY: Do you ever look up and say, "Wow, I was walking around up there!"?

IRWIN: I look up there and say, "Man, that's where I went for my summer vacation in '71!" It's easy to pick out our landing spot.

ANTHONY: Can you see it looking at the moon from here?

IRWIN: Yes.

ANTHONY: What would you tell someone to look for?

IRWIN: I tell people it's between the eyes of the man in the moon. In fact, it's right on his nose.

ANTHONY: I've heard you say that everyone who has been on the moon—everyone who has been in space, in fact—has had some kind of spiritual recognition of something beyond themselves. But in your case there was a spiritual recognition that was attached to responsibilities, a recognition of the reality of Christ. And now you've become what might be termed an evangelist. Do you think of yourself as an evangelist?

IRWIN: Not really. I'm afraid if I use that word people will consider me to be a frustrated preacher, and some people would turn me off. I would rather be considered as a guy who has had a very unique experience and just likes to tell what happened. I like to share with people and let them listen with an open mind and assess whether it is something that makes sense to them.

ANTHONY: Let's assume you are talking to an audience of about ten-thousand people, and none of them are Christians. In sharing what happened to you, in a couple of minutes, what would you tell them?

IRWIN: Depending on the time I would have, I would tell them about the things I saw on the flight. One thing that was important to me was the view of the earth. We could look back and see it as just a very small ball in the sky; actually, it looked about the size of a basketball. It was a unique opportunity to view the earth from that perspective. It looked like the most fragile, delicate Christmas tree ornament you could imagine. It looked as if you just were to touch it with your finger it would crumble and fall apart.

The second most impressive thing was to see the spaceship Earth shrink in size from the size of a basketball down to the size of a baseball, then to the size of a golf ball, and finally to the size of a marble. That experience has to change a person inside. It has to make him truly appreciate everything we have here on this earth. It has to make a man appreciate the creation of God, the love of God, and the infinite precision with which He controls everything out in space, and of course everything here on the earth, too. But we lose sight of that as we sit here on the earth, because we feel so comfortable and so secure we don't realize we're on a spaceship traveling sixty thousand miles an hour. It's not until you're in a very small spaceship destined for a rendezvous with another heavenly body that is traveling thousands of miles an hour that you realize everything is in perfect order. While on the surface of the moon and seeing that beautiful sight, there was a feeling of being aware of the power and the presence of another being that I have never experienced for that duration here on the earth. I talk a lot about the presence of God, because I don't know any other words to use.

Then of course, one of the very moving things which occurred while on the moon was finding the Genesis rock, the white rock. We were looking for it, but never dreamed we would find it presented to us in such a clear and unique way. We were able to see it long before we got over to where it was held up and presented to us on a pedestal, and there was no doubt it was the rock we had hoped to find. Again, it seemed to be God's hand guiding us to that rock so we could bring it back. It's the only pure white rock which has been brought back from the moon; it is the oldest rock that has been age-dated in the universe. But as I got back to our lunar module that night, the Falcon, and prepared to go to sleep, I prayed and reflected on the day and just thanked God for His guidance, because it seemed that He had indeed led us right to that spot.

ANTHONY: What is the significance of the Genesis rock? What was it you were looking for?

IRWIN: We were looking for a rock that represented the mountains of the moon. The mountains of the moon represent material that came from a deeper level, thrown out when these large craters were formed. So it would represent probably the oldest material on the moon. We were told before we went to look for white or light-colored rock. They knew it had to be light both in color and in density. When you look at the moon through a telescope, the mountains or the highlands are generally lighter than the basins or the mare surfaces. They also knew from analyzing the dark rocks, the basaltic rocks that had previously been brought back from the moon, that the moon could not be entirely made up of that type of material or it would be too heavy to be in its present orbit. So they knew that a lighter rock had to exist, and we were instructed to look for this type of rock. We never realized we would find it so easily, because most of the rocks are covered with dust. But that wasn't so with this rock. It was labeled the Genesis rock before we ever brought it back, because some of those men realized the significance of the rock.

ANTHONY: I suppose in every culture or every society that has ever been on the earth, men have dreamed of walking on the moon. You had some time and some freedom when you were just bouncing around that one-sixth gravity; what were some of your thoughts and reflections at that time, or were you too busy setting up the seismometers?

IRWIN: Well, there wasn't a great deal of time for reflection, very little in fact. When we were outside the spacecraft we had a limited supply of water and oxygen, and all our time was programmed. We were supposed to be doing something, making verbal observations of what we saw, and there was very little time to reflect on how we felt. We really were on the moon, but frankly, most of the time we couldn't convince ourselves that we were because we were in familiar terrain. We were surrounded by mountains, and we had trained in that type of terrain for several years before the flight, so it was like we were on a training expedition. It was difficult to realize we were a quarter of a million miles away from the home base. The force of gravity on the moon is less than on earth, of course, so that we did feel light, but we had simulated that very well here on the earth.

The only way we could truly convince ourselves that we were on the moon and not on the earth was to look directly overhead, and there was the earth about the size of a marble. But in order to do that we had to look directly overhead, and we had to have something to hold onto, because we were already off-balance with our big heavy back-packs on. To lean back without anything to hold onto would cause us to fall over on our backs, which we did a few times. I only had a couple of opportunities to look up in the sky to see the earth. Even when we would wake up in the morning it was usually a hassle to get ready for the day. Fortunately, when we would lie down on our hammocks after the day's operation, then we would have a chance to reflect and say a prayer before we drifted into sleep. A few times I would wake up during the night, during a rest period, and reflect a little bit before I would go back to sleep.

ANTHONY: When you woke up during the night, did you know where you were immediately in that instant of waking?

IRWIN: Well, I knew I was in the lunar module, and I had to think for a moment, "Is this the simulation again?" Actually, we had simulated the sleep situation here on the earth, because there is quite a bit of noise inside the lunar module from the pumps and the fans. We were wondering if we would be able to sleep. So we simulated that for many, many evenings and actually slept the whole night in the lunar module. So I would wake up and wonder, "Is this simulation again, or is it for real?"

ANTHONY: Jim, I understand you came to the Lord as a young boy, and then as young boys often do, you strayed away.

IRWIN: That's right. I grew up in a Christian home and a Christian atmosphere. I made that decision for Christ when I was eleven years old at a revival service. Then our family began moving around the country, but I was still going to church. I went to the Naval Academy, then joined the Air Force and really started moving around. It was during that time that I strayed from going to church, because airplanes and flying became an obsession with me. I was flying all the time. Of course that is what led me to go into the astronaut program. I was always trying to fly a little higher and a little faster. One day I would fly airplanes, and another day I would fly spacecraft, and there was not much time at all for spiritual development.

ANTHONY: But during this time on the moon there was obviously a change in your life. I've talked to people who knew you before and after the trip, and it was obvious to those around you that something had happened, something had changed you. Can you remember a specific instance when there was a recognition of the deeper revelation of Christ, or was it a combination of things?

IRWIN: It was a result of the total experience—the twelve days being removed from the earth and seeing those things that I shall never see again. I came back with a new appreciation for the earth, and the human beings on the earth, and a deep love for the Creator, God, who was there with us.

ANTHONY: What about your family? I was in the service, and knew many pilots. It seemed there were always family troubles because of the way of living, or the separation, or something. Was there a bringing together of your family after you got back this time?

IRWIN: Yes, there was, because I took them on trips with me after the flight, and they understood what I was trying to do. I was trying to share the experience and really bring everyone into a closer relationship with the Lord. My wife and our five children became great partners in that venture. My wife is a very strong witness to her faith, but the children are strong too. They each have their own testimony.

ANTHONY: Seeing their dad on television walking around on the moon must have affected their lives.

IRWIN: No, it really didn't. In fact, it was difficult for my wife to get them to watch television. They would much rather go out and play with the other kids in the neighborhood. But at one point she did force them to come in off the street and watch their dad on television. By the time I went to the moon it was old hat. Some of the other guys in the neighborhood had been on the moon, so the kids accepted it as though I was going to work across the street. It was no big deal to them.

ANTHONY: I remember you quoted a Scripture that was carried in the press.

IRWIN: I tried to quote Scripture, and it was a rather feeble attempt; it was the first time I had ever tried to quote Scripture.

ANTHONY: What was it, do you remember?

IRWIN: "I will lift up mine eyes unto the hills, from whence cometh my help" (Psalm 121:1).

ANTHONY: That was when you were driving that little land rover?

IRWIN: Yes. It was a beautiful morning, and it was as if we were just out for a little Sunday drive. Dave and I were remarking about the beauty of that particular morning, looking up at the mountains. He just opened the way and set the stage perfectly for me to try to quote Scripture, and it was all completely unrehearsed. But I did tack on the statement that we were getting a lot of help from Houston, because I didn't want those guys to turn off the radio!

ANTHONY: Did you know there were Christian wagers made here on earth that you wouldn't be able to name that Scripture when you got back?

IRWIN: I can see you've been talking to some of my friends!

ANTHONY: Yes, the other astronauts in the program, the others who have walked on the moon. It seems to me the Lord has chosen you for something special, something different. Do you feel that? Do you feel a burden on your life or a responsibility that some of us don't have?

IRWIN: Yes, I do. Looking back on my life, there were so many problems, so many accidents and near-tragedies.

ANTHONY: Were you a fighter pilot?

IRWIN: Yes, I was a fighter pilot and test pilot most of the time. I had a very serious accident in which I was severely injured. There was a question as to whether I would ever walk again, let alone fly. And it just seemed to be in the cards that I would never be a test pilot and certainly not an astronaut, let alone have the opportunity to go to the moon. But I did have that opportunity, and looking back on it, I think it was part of the Lord's plan for me that He would allow me to go that far away and come back just to serve Him. Really, the greatest mission I could ever undertake is just to share the experience of His greatness and the smallness but important nature of man.

ANTHONY: Sometimes people, when they're very young, have had an almost mysterious knowledge or a foretaste that something was going to be different in their lives, and it made them different all the way through. I've talked to people who experienced this at the age of three or five. Did you ever experience that?

IRWIN: Yes, when I was that age I would look at the moon and tell whoever was there at the time that I was going to go there someday.

ANTHONY: Did you really believe it?

IRWIN: Apparently I believed it at the time, but then as I developed a little more I lost that confidence I had had when I was five or eight years old. But I guess I said it with a great deal of confidence at a young age.

ANTHONY: The Lord had probably given you some

foretaste of what would happen. That seems to be His style, from what I can see in my life. He is probably showing you something that it is hard for you to talk about that is a foretaste of what is going to happen to you in the next few years. It's almost as if He's preparing the way. This is an area that is hard to talk about, but do you know what I mean?

IRWIN: I know what you're saying, and I do feel in the deepest way that He does have a purpose for me, and I think the High Flight Foundation is part of that purpose. But I think He's still preparing me for exactly what He wants me to do. I still have difficulty articulating feelings. Frankly, before the flight I hated public speaking, really dreaded it. I couldn't sleep for several nights before a speaking date. But I think it was a gift from the Lord that He did give me something He wanted me to share with people, and I enjoyed public speaking after I got back from the flight.

ANTHONY: Jim, I've seen your book; did you write it as soon as you got back from the trip to the moon?

IRWIN: No, actually, I started that after I retired. *To Rule The Night* is the title of the book. It seemed appropriate that the title should come from the Scriptures, although it did take us quite awhile to come up with an appropriate title. But one night my writer and my wife and I were looking through the Bible and we came across those words in Genesis 1:16. They seemed so appropriate, and they just seemed to leap off the page at us. On the fourth day God did create two great lights: the greater light to rule the day and the lesser light to rule the night.

The book is really an autobiography, but it includes a great deal about the trip to the moon, and the preparation of the men for the trip. The trip is described in very human terms, so hopefully everyone feels like they're on the trip themselves and experiencing some of the things I experienced. I have this feeling of obligation and responsibility to tell people what I saw and what I felt. It's all there in the book. It's about Jim Irwin's flight to that lesser light, the moon. But it's more than that; it's a story of another light, the light of Christ that can come into anyone's life and illuminate their darkest hours, to rule their night. It's a rather mysterious title that tells a story that is really the key to life itself.

ANTHONY: Is it available in bookstores anywhere?

IRWIN: If it's a good bookstore it should have the book! Also, the book is available from High Flight.

ANTHONY: The High Flight Foundation, 4050 American Drive, Colorado Springs, Colorado 80907. This foundation is something you founded as a thrust to share an experience with others. The most exciting and newsworthy thing High Flight did was the P.O.W. retreats after they returned from Viet Nam. What led you to get into that?

IRWIN: That moon flight was the greatest trip I had ever taken, and I wanted to tell people about it, so I started doing that. I spent every weekend traveling around the country sharing the experience, usually speaking in churches. Weekends were the busiest part of my week. I took my family with me as a rule. Then I had the opportunity to retire, and it seemed like the Lord opened the door for me to be able to do full-time what I had only been able to do part-time.

But I knew I couldn't do it by myself; I needed others to help me. So that is why I agreed to establish a foundation with a nucleus of dedicated people to share their faith. We chose the name High Flight Foundation based on the poem entitled, "High Flight," written by a young aviator. It captures the imagination of high flight, but most importantly, we want everyone to have a high flight as they live their lives on this earth, and ultimately to make the very highest flight. Initially, the foundation was to enable me to travel. But it has become more than that. It has become a foundation which enables other people to share their faith.

The foundation also tries to serve, in unique ways, as many people as we can on the earth. We hope to share with them on a person-to-person basis, but sometimes that is not always possible. Occasionally we invite people to come to the mountains for a retreat to get away from the busy world and to come to a spiritual renewal experience. We had the retreat for the prisoners of war and families of the M.I.A.'s (missing in action) last summer. That occurred because we knew the prisoners were being released.

Our executive director and vice president, Bill Rittenhouse, was a prisoner of war during the Second World War in Rumania. So he had insight and feeling for what these guys would go through when they came back to their loved ones. So naturally he asked the question, "What is the country going to do for them?" And we found out nothing was going to be done on a national basis to help them in a spiritual way through the trauma of meeting a wife who had changed over five or six years, perhaps children whom they had never even known. So we had a lot of encouragement from the Department of Defense and also the League of Missing In Action Families, and we decided we would take it on as a foundation project. We invited all of them and their families, because we wanted it to be an opportunity for the families to draw closer together and know God and know Christ. The Department of Defense and the National League sent out the invitations, and we merely provided the staff and invited other personalities from around the country to come in and share with them. And it was really a great experience, because we saw lives dramatically changed and families put back together.

ANTHONY: Jim, would you read the poem for the

audience?

IRWIN: Gladly, if they take into consideration that I am not normally a reader of poetry.

"HIGH FLIGHT"
Oh, I have slipped the surly bonds of earth,
And danced the skies on laughter-silvered wings;
Sunward I've climbed and joined the tumbling mirth
    of sun-split clouds—and done a hundred things
You have not dreamed of—wheeled and soared and
        swung
High in the sunlit silence. Hovering there
I've chased the shouting wind along and flung
My eager craft through footless halls of air
Up, up the long delirious burning blue
I've topped the wind-swept heights with easy grace,
Where never lark, or even eagle, flew;
And, while with silent, lifting mind I've trod
The high untrespassed sanctity of space,
Put out my hand, and touched the face of God.

ANTHONY: Who is the author, Jim?

IRWIN: He was a young aviator killed in a mid-air collision early in World War II. His mother was English and his father was an American. He was from the same town I was—Pittsburgh. He wrote many other inspirational poems, but none that are as well-known as that particular one. His name is John Gillespie Magee, Jr.

ANTHONY: You've got to know that someone who really loved flying wrote that poem, which is probably why you liked it yourself.

IRWIN: All aviators are familiar with it, and I think even people who are earth-bound can relate to it and understand what he is trying to say.

ANTHONY: What was the single most memorable experience during the whole P.O.W. and M.I.A. retreat?

IRWIN: Well, I think the most dramatic example of the Lord working in the lives of those people was a husband and wife coming together. Here was a couple who came into the retreat situation and were not even speaking to each other. They were so hostile to each other they even asked for separate rooms. And to see their lives changed almost in the twinkling of an eye, to see the woman break down and sob and then go and actually hold her husband's hand, and for the rest of the retreat to walk around like newlyweds—that was something we just didn't dream was possible. We knew the situation existed before they even came in, so we were in prayer about it. And we shared with them and prayed with them after they got there. But we never expected such a dramatic change in two people's lives. We received mail from them, and we even received a very generous contribution. They said High Flight was the high point in their lives, because it had meant so much to them.

ANTHONY: Did you have almost all the prisoners of war and their families there?

IRWIN: No, not really. We had almost fifteen-hundred people, but we had only about twenty-five P.O.W.'s and their families. By last summer already seventy percent of the prisoners had divorced or separated, so they were no longer with their families. Not too many P.O.W. families stayed together.

ANTHONY: People don't know that, do they?

IRWIN: Probably not. Of those prisoners who were still with their families, we had about forty percent or fifty percent of them. Many of them had made previous commitments, and there were some who frankly didn't see the need for a spiritual retreat.

ANTHONY: You're planning to sponsor another retreat; is it the same thing?

IRWIN: This summer, because of the press of time and other things we want to do, we only have two weeks to make available for a retreat. We're inviting those who were unable to come last summer, because we had to turn away about six-hundred families who wanted to come. This summer we hope to take care of many of them.

ANTHONY: Do you personally feel a hurt to try to be an instrument of cohesiveness in bringing families back together? Where does Jim Irwin hurt most for the world?

IRWIN: That's a new question!

ANTHONY: Is that the first new question I've asked all night?

IRWIN: No! I hate to see people lost and searching for a plan for their lives, because I believe God does have a plan and purpose for each one of us. And it goes beyond the individual; it goes to the family. I think the family unit can provide a harmony to allow those youngsters to grow up with a sense of purpose for their lives. I just hate to see broken families.

ANTHONY: Let me put you back on the moon for a moment, okay? Many people repeat memorized Scriptures and they have just become rote. Paul said something I would like you to respond to and relate to the time when you were on the moon. Paul said, "For me to live is Christ" (Philippians 1:21). He also said, "I am crucified with Christ: nevertheless I live; yet not I, but Christ liveth in me . . . " (Galatians 2:20). What does that mean to you?

IRWIN: If Christ is part of our lives, then He will shine through and people will see Christ as we live. As God worked in Christ, He can work in us so people can see that this man has been transformed and that he is different.

ANTHONY: Other people saw a change in you, and you may not have even recognized it. He probably changed you without your knowing it in many ways. Did the knowledge of that Scripture—"For me to live is

Christ''—really grab you? Could you relate to that?

IRWIN: I can relate to it very strongly.

ANTHONY: Could you put flying on the altar now and never fly again?

IRWIN: Yes, I could. My love was flying, but it seems that I can serve the Lord better not to fly, by conserving that energy to share my faith. And of course He put me in that position with the heart attack I had about a year ago.

ANTHONY: I understand that it was a very serious heart attack.

IRWIN: No one was more surprised than I was.

ANTHONY: But you have to be in perfect health to be in the astronaut program.

IRWIN: Well, I've always been a physical fitness nut, you know, and I was always trying to take care of myself. But I must confess that I figured if I was able to go to the moon I was superhuman and could do anything. I found out as a result of that experience that I am just as fragile as the rest of the human beings here on the earth.

ANTHONY: Do you think God was showing you something?

IRWIN: Yes, I'm sure He was. My wife tells me He wanted me to take a vacation and a short rest, because I was really pushing myself. I was really not spending much time at all at home. I was sacrificing my home life for this new mission. And I think having a heart attack enabled me to reevaluate priorities and to spend more time with my family, and to make sure when I do go out for speaking engagements that they're important.

ANTHONY: Another organization I know about tried for eighteen months to get you to speak for them. For eighteen months they wrote letters, and only two days ago I got the idea, "It would be nice to have Jim Irwin on the show." I'm glad it didn't take eighteen months to get you.

IRWIN: Well, the Lord works in mysterious ways!

ANTHONY: Let's go back to something else. You went into the astronaut program in 1966, and even before that your life had been disciplined. Has the training and discipline helped you in disciplining and learning to yield to God? We in the Body of Christ often don't have enough discipline to yield our wills to Him, because we're so into our routine habit patterns. But it seems to me that you are blessed with all that training and discipline, and if you can direct it to Him, it's got to be unique.

IRWIN: I pray every day that it is directed for Him, and for His purpose, but occasionally I am sure I stumble and have the same falls as other human beings who were not always completely receptive, completely directed by Him. That is a problem common to all of us.

ANTHONY: You said earlier that if you can go to the moon you can do anything. But when you were in the astronaut program, as a group you had to sort of look down on the rest of us poor mortals. There must be a built-in pride. Most of us would never have to have that temptation.

IRWIN: That's true. I guess I've always been rather proud.

ANTHONY: But I don't sense any pride in you now. It's strange.

IRWIN: Well, I hope I am not proud to the same degree as before. I am proud that I am a Christian.

ANTHONY: But how do you deal with pride? You're always the center of attention wherever you go; you're one of twelve men in the entire world who has walked on the moon. Now to the natural man, that has got to build up Jim Irwin's ego. How do you deal with that?

IRWIN: I keep telling myself that it is part of the Lord's plan for me. If I have any fame or publicity or recognition it is only to serve Him, because people will listen to me. They may listen only out of curiosity, but they will at least listen to what I have to say, and so I view it as the opportunity of a lifetime. Some people might say I'm trying to use my moon experience for my own purposes, but I am using it for the Lord's purpose. And that is why I'm involved with High Flight.

ANTHONY: Have you had much experience speaking in other countries?

IRWIN: Yes, I have. I've had the opportunity to travel on almost every continent on the earth since I got back from the moon.

ANTHONY: Have you spoken in Russia?

IRWIN: No, unfortunately I haven't been in Russia. The only Iron Countries I've been to are Poland and Yugoslavia.

ANTHONY: In those countries did you get a chance to talk about the love and the grace of God? You were still in the service then, weren't you?

IRWIN: Yes, I was, but the circumstances were rather unusual. On a visit to Yugoslavia I did have an opportunity to speak in St. Paul's Cathedral in Belgrade. I shared a testimony there, but it was the first time I had ever had that opportunity in a foreign country.

ANTHONY: When did you leave the service?

IRWIN: I retired in August, 1972, after a little over twenty-one years of service.

ANTHONY: Since you've been in High Flight have you traveled much with the direct purpose of witnessing? Have you been to Africa?

IRWIN: That's the one continent I have never visited. I would like to go to Africa and I have tentative plans to go to South Africa this fall.

ANTHONY: In the Muslim religion, part of their belief was that it would be impossible for man to ever walk on the moon. I don't know this for a fact, but I understand one of the reasons for the great spiritual revolution that is sweeping Africa now through the Muslim countries is that they heard and saw that you walked on the moon. So, indirectly, you may have been responsible for hundreds of thousands of people coming to the Lord. Do you realize that?

IRWIN: I knew the moon was holy to the Muslims, but I didn't know they believed man would not be allowed to walk on the moon. Of course, a lot of our people believe that too!

ANTHONY: In the Buck Rogers comic books and the movies you see about astronauts, at the moment of lift-off you see the skin go back and the tremendous G-forces on you so you can't move. Is that what happens?

IRWIN: It does, but it takes about a minute before the G-forces build up. But it's just a four-G level.

ANTHONY: You can still blink your eyes, for example?

IRWIN: You can, but it takes some effort to move your hand to move a switch or circuit breaker. The really high G-force is when we come back into the atmosphere. Then it gets up to about seven G's and it would be almost impossible to lift your hand at that point.

ANTHONY: I wonder if you know fear. You probably know what apprehension is, but do you know what fear is? Have you ever experienced fear?

IRWIN: I've known fear—fear for my own life, fear for my own safety.

ANTHONY: As an astronaut?

IRWIN: No, I never knew fear as an astronaut. But right after I became a test pilot I had that very serious aircraft accident, and for some reason that accident removed any fear.

ANTHONY: What is the difference between fear and apprehension?

IRWIN: I think just degree.

ANTHONY: I'm just thinking of you lying in that little tiny bubble on top of that monstrous rocket with thousands of pounds of fuel in it that could explode and really send you somewhere, and you spend a lot of time lying there thinking about it. It's got to be freaky, thinking about a lot of things like that.

IRWIN: Yes, you do think about a lot of things. You wonder, "I've gone this far. How did I get here?" After you finally enter the craft, the hours drag by, because there is not much for you to do except look at the instruments and listen to the countdown. But in those last minutes time moves very, very fast and before you know it you hear the word "ignition," and then you sense and hear and feel all that tremendous power that is beginning to lift you off the earth. There is a moment of supreme elation, complete release of tension. That was almost the happiest moment of my life to realize that after all these years of training and preparation, at last it was my turn. At last I'm leaving the earth. In fact, I would like all people to know the thrill of leaving the earth, and they can look forward to that.

ANTHONY: Do you think you got a foretaste of what the feeling of rapture may be?

IRWIN: I'm sure I did.

ANTHONY: Twenty-five thousand miles an hour! That's pretty fast, isn't it?

IRWIN: That's pretty fast, but we will probably move much faster in our spiritual state.

ANTHONY: In our new bodies without spacesuits, in the twinkling of an eye . . . .

IRWIN: We'll probably be going faster than the speed of light.

JOHNNY GARCIA

This is a man who looks like a panther. A movie called **The Dirty Dozen** portrays his and some of his compatriots' activities in the Second World War. Trained to kill during his military service, he later killed a policeman, then killed his cellmate. He was a heroin addict, a hardened criminal. But a small child's love and simple faith penetrated his stony heart, and he met God. His heart's desire was to return to prison so he could share with those in need. He now has his heart's desire, and he has caused a revolution in the California prison systems. Listen to an unusual story.

CHAPTER 9

JOHNNY GARCIA

After killing Germans in the war, then a policeman, then my cellmate, I couldn't believe God could forgive me—but He has!

ANTHONY: A lot of people use their own evil as an excuse for not coming to God. But Jesus said, "The one who comes to Me I will certainly not cast out" (John 6:37). That Scripture verse means He *never* rejects one who comes to Him, no matter what their past has been. Otherwise He would have turned Johnny Garcia away.

Johnny Garcia spent twenty-two years in prison. I am sure there is not another man in the whole world who has been seven times under death sentence for killing a policeman, as Johnny was at San Quentin. Three times they put him inside the gas chamber at San Quentin, ready to drop the cyanide pellets into the acid vat. In each case, just a few moments before they were to drop the pellets, his life was spared by a phone call from the governor.

After he was released from prison he went back on drugs again, but at the end of 1972 Johnny was converted and wonderfully transformed by Jesus. He turned himself into the police because they had charges against him. He offered to face his record, whatever the penalty, and he begged them to send him to Folsom Prison so he could witness to the prisoners who need Jesus there. They gave him six months in the county jail in Los Angeles. God turned that jail inside out with revival, and it spread from there to the prisons all over California.

Why didn't they execute Johnny? Two reasons: God's mercy, and because as a teenager he had joined the armed forces. He volunteered for special service and while in France won not only a Presidential citation, but a lieutenant's commission. He was in his late teens at that time. Because he was a hero with a great war record, they changed his death sentence and made it life imprisonment. But God was behind it all.

Johnny has a story to tell. He knows Jesus Christ in a personal way, a way in which not nearly enough Christians know Him.

Johnny, you were just released from prison a few days ago, is that right?

GARCIA: Yes, from the Los Angeles County Jail.

ANTHONY: You said something amazing when I heard you speak a little while ago. You said you want to go back there. Why do you want to go back to jail?

GARCIA: The reason for wanting to go back is because I saw what is needed there, and I saw the power of God and the Holy Spirit moving in that jail. I know the comfort the Holy Spirit was to certain individuals who were under heavy sentences and on their way to the state prisons. After finding Jesus they went gladly, because they knew they now had something they had never had before in their lives. They promised to go and spread the Word and share with others what they had experienced there in the county jail.

ANTHONY: It's not often one gets an opportunity to talk to someone who has the testimony and reality of Christ that is in your life. What is in your heart right now?

GARCIA: What is in my heart right now is the love of God that He has put there. My intention, if the Lord wishes, is that I want to be used by Him, because of the many sins He has forgiven me. Like He says in the Bible, "Go into all the world and preach the gospel to the whole creation" (Mark 16:15). This is something I believe should be done in the darkest places on the face of the earth, where there is no one else to go. There are people who will go into the prisons, but the prisoners will not listen, because the ones who go to spread the Word haven't been in their shoes. And I feel a prison ministry should be ministered by one who has been there. This is the burden I feel now, and I ask my Lord to allow me to work for Him in that field.

ANTHONY: When you were in San Quentin you were physically walked down the aisle ready to be put into the gas chamber seven times?

GARCIA: That's right.

ANTHONY: Three times you were strapped into the chair ready for the cyanide pellets to be released?

GARCIA: Yes, on three different occasions.

ANTHONY: That must have scared you a little bit.

GARCIA: Yes, it did.

ANTHONY: This was all before you were a Christian?

GARCIA: Yes.

ANTHONY: What did you feel? When you were sitting there and you knew that tablet was about to be released, what was your thought?

GARCIA: Well, part of the time my mind was blank. Part of the time I went all the way back into my earliest childhood and remembered things I did with my mother, things I did with my father, things that happened in my young life. It was like a rerun of my whole life. I am sweating now, but you can imagine how I was sweating then!

ANTHONY: Did you have any inkling before you accepted Christ that there was something you were going to do? Did you have any confidence that you were going to be saved? Or did you know you were going to die?

GARCIA: I felt I was going to die. But all through my life I've had a hole in my gut where the wind was blowing through. I tried to solve that and tried to cover that hole through narcotics, through drink, through women, through guns, through joining different organizations of crime, and nothing worked. The only one who has helped is the Great Physician. He has taken over and has stopped up this hole in my gut.

ANTHONY: So you tried everything. Did you try heroin?

GARCIA: Oh yes, heroin.

ANTHONY: You were hooked on heroin?

GARCIA: I've been hooked on heroin several times. I had my first fix in 1938 at the age of thirteen. When I came out of prison I was hooked on it again. I was hooked on it when I was pulling those robberies where the policeman was killed. And when I came out of prison I went directly to heroin again. I went back to prison and came out again, and went back to narcotics again. The last time I got out of state prison, before the county jail, I was hooked again, and I hung up my parole. That means I wasn't reporting to my parole officer. I was hooked on narcotics, and a policeman in Los Angeles asked me if I would make a buy for him, and I burnt him for the money.

ANTHONY: That means you ripped him off!

GARCIA: Yes, and the guy I was supposed to set up for him told me that policeman said he wasn't going to arrest me; he was going to kill me. On September 13, 1972, I was in a phone booth making a call to a narcotics connection. When I came out of the phone booth I heard a shot and it seemed like a bird went by my ear. I looked across the street and there was that policeman sitting in his car holding his wrist and he had his gun in his hand. I saw the flash of the second shot and I turned and started to run. I had a jacket on and had the collar up. I heard the third shot, but I was moving then. A bullet hit my collar and made a hole in it. I jumped a fence. It was unbelievable. I don't believe a world champion pole vaulter could make that jump. But I did it without a pole!

A few days after that I called up Fellowship Vine in Pasadena and talked to Nick Cadena who is the director there. I asked him if I could come over to kick my heroin habit. He said, "Yes, come on over."

When I got there I told him I was hot, that I had hung some stuff.

ANTHONY: That's the understatement of the year!

GARCIA: He accepted me, and told me we would talk about all this other after I had kicked my habit. The main thing was for me to get my mind straightened out. At that home a week later, on September 22nd, I received the first birthday cake I had ever received in my life.

Nick has four girls, and the baby is three years old. On the third day I was sitting in a chair on the back lawn. All of a sudden it felt as if someone had hit me in the solar plexus and I bent over in great pain. Withdrawal from heroin is very painful! I heard Nick's wife, Pauline, say to the little baby, "Look, Johnny is sick. Go out there and pray for him." I heard this little baby's footsteps running toward me, but I couldn't look up because I was bent over in pain.

This little baby put her hand on my forehead and started to pray for me. All she could say was, "Amen, amen, amen." There was a warm feeling that came over my body that is unexplainable. It was like when you are cold and somebody wraps you in a warm blanket, it was a warmth that was out of this world. It came from out of this world through that baby. The withdrawal pains left immediately.

I had told Nick Cadena that I was never going to cry. I had seen many people there who were crying when they had services, and I asked, "What is all the crying about?"

He said, "Well, that is the love of the Lord." But I couldn't understand it. I said, "I'm going to turn this Bible back to the Lord if He ever makes me cry."

A month and a half later we went down near San Diego to a little town called Fallbrook. They called me up to give a testimony there, and I was telling them the same thing I am telling you. But when I got to this part about the little baby praying for someone like me, that broke me and I wept. God used that little baby to soften this granite heart. He showed me what pure love is.

ANTHONY: It's something we will never understand, isn't it? It's a mystery, something we call "amazing grace."

But there was the time when you were in the gas chamber, knowing that cyanide capsule was about to come down, knowing you had killed a policeman. Later you killed your cellmate?

GARCIA: I killed my cellmate approximately two months after coming off death row.

ANTHONY: Nobody can understand that. But God understands it, doesn't He? When you look back at your life now, how do you feel about it?

GARCIA: I regret, naturally, some of the things that have happened, because of the hurt I realize now was dealt out to the families of these people. Those are the things I regret, knowing what I realize now. But at the time I couldn't care less. I wasn't with Jesus and I was blind and completely lost. I had no respect for law or for life. I had seen a lot of lives lost during World War II, and it meant nothing to me. It was just a case of being here today and gone tomorrow.

ANTHONY: There's a Scripture that has become my favorite. "And we know that all things work together for good to them that love God, to them who are called according to His purpose." That means everything in the whole universe!

GARCIA: That is Romans 8:28.

ANTHONY: How many times have you heard the "yes, but" Christians? "Well, that's a good Scripture, but . . . . " But it is *all things*. And that's the confidence we have in Him. Even your life can work for good to those who love the Lord and are called according to His purpose.

GARCIA: I believe that sincerely, with all of my heart.

ANTHONY: You know it, don't you? It's not just understanding.

GARCIA: I know it; I've felt it; I've tasted it. I'm alive in it now.

ANTHONY: You've got to have a little feeling about this policeman who was committed to kill you. If he sees you right now he's liable to shoot you!

GARCIA: That has already been taken care of. He knows in case something does happen that he would be accused. And he knows what I'm doing; he knows about the revival and the fellows who were saved in the county jail. He's got a pretty good understanding. But when you work in the narcotic division, you know that the narcotic addict is a liar, a cheat. I suppose he is one of the lowest creatures that could be walking the streets. They've got quite a job to do. I know I ripped him off, but he had his reasons for doing what he was doing.

ANTHONY: Have you talked to him?

GARCIA: Yes, I've talked to him through people who know him personally. This is something that I want to write about, and I want him to be with me when this is brought to light.

ANTHONY: You were telling me before about an amazing Scripture you found in the book of Job. For some reason, you said you could identify with Job. Share that Scripture, remembering that you were in death row, seven times headed for the gas chamber.

GARCIA: I want to tell you how it happened. I didn't

quite understand that I could be forgiven for my sins when I accepted the Lord into my heart. There was doubt in my natural mind that God would forgive a sinner of my caliber. Paul said that he was a chief sinner. Well, he's got other chiefs with him now. I told Nick one day it was hard for me to believe the Lord had really forgiven me. He said, "I'm going to call somebody up and I want you to talk to this fellow. He's going to tell you about his life and what happened."

My friend, Joe Donato, came over to the house and I met him. Joe had me open the Bible to 1 John 1:9: "If we confess our sins, He is faithful and just to forgive us our sins, and to cleanse us from *all* unrighteousness." Then he explained that Scripture to me, and told me about his life and how he believed our Lord had forgiven him. I wanted to believe, and I told the Lord, "Lord, I want to believe, and they say you don't tell even one single little lie in this Book." Some books inform, other books reform, but this is the only book that *transforms!*

I was reading the book of Job because I had heard the people at Fellowship Vine talking about Job and how he had had everything taken away from him, yet he didn't turn against God. He didn't utter even one word against the Lord, and then everything was restored to him. And as I read I came upon this Scripture in Job 5:19, 20: "From six troubles He will deliver you, even in seven, evil will not touch you. In famine He will redeem you from death: and in war from the power of the sword." This is true: He did all of this for me!

ANTHONY: That Scripture was written thousands of years ago, but it was written for Johnny Garcia!

GARCIA: I believe that sincerely. This jumped right out at me, and I went running to several of the brothers and sisters at Fellowship Vine and said, "Look what it says here!" Joe had given me a Bible he had signed, which another ex-con owns now. I had marked it in there, and the next time Joe came over I showed it to him and said, "Look how there's something in here for everyone!" He read it and said, "Yes, it's true."

ANTHONY: Did you ever meet any members of the Mafia when you were on the street?

GARCIA: Yes, I met several people connected with the Mafia. I've done business with them. We used to steal adding machines and they would buy them from us.

ANTHONY: The Mafia organization is very much looked up to in the world of crime, isn't it?

GARCIA: Very much so, especially by youngsters who like the flashy clothes and the flashy cars and the flashy girls. The young people always look up to the kingpins of the underworld.

ANTHONY: If four or five key figures in the underworld were to give their lives to the Lord, that could have a tremendous impact in the crime world, couldn't it?

GARCIA: It certainly would. I know that other hearts would be touched who are lost in the underworld. I believe there is a lot of intelligence in the underworld characters. If they could realize the tremendous change and the tremendous peace that comes by having the Lord in your heart—like Joe Donato says, you can pay ten thousand dollars for a bed, but you can't buy sleep. You can't go into Neiman/Marcus here in Dallas and say, "I want ten thousand dollars worth of happiness."

ANTHONY: I've known a lot of criminals in my lifetime, and there is so much fear tied up in that way of life. There is no peace whatsoever.

GARCIA: There is always the apprehension that somebody wants to take your place and step up there. There is always someone behind you trying to get to your niche all the way to the top. There is always greediness and envy.

ANTHONY: But the same thing is true in the business world. A friend of mine had a high position in a big motor corporation, and he left organized business for the same reasons you left the underworld. It was strangling him.

The prisoner or the guy in the Mafia will not accept the philosophy that Christ was a nice man or that He was a good philosopher or something. What they will accept is the power of God.

GARCIA: We have to step out there with faith, and we have to show them that God is alive. The only way we can show them God is alive is by showing them the miracles God can and does perform, and will perform if we ask Him.

ANTHONY: You know, a miracle is the common denominator that can reach all people. No one can close his eyes to a miracle.

Johnny, you joined the army when you were sixteen years old, and it set the stage for a lot of things that happened in your later life, didn't it?

GARCIA: Amen. Jesus does plan. He is the greatest planner in the universe.

ANTHONY: A couple years after you went into the service you got a battlefield commission, and a Presidential citation, and these were the tools the Lord ended up using many years later. Share that part of your life with us.

GARCIA: I came out of a special school for boys when I was sixteen and I joined the United States Army. I went to Fort McLellan, Alabama, for basic training. When I finished the six weeks of training there, a lieutenant in charge of paratroopers came over and asked if there was anybody who wanted to volunteer for the paratroopers. I stepped forward, as did many others. We were taken to Fort Benning, Georgia, and went to jump school training there. Then we were put on a boat and sent to England.

In England they asked for twenty-six volunteers for some hazardous duty, and I stepped forward. I felt that if I was going to fight I wanted to be right in the middle of the worst of the fight. I was a youngster and I was all fired up. I had pledged absolute allegiance to my country, and I also felt I had to do what had to be done—I wanted to be a part of it. They took all twenty-six of us to a special compound away from everybody else and gave us special training. They built a building for us exactly like the one we were going to enter in France. At the time we didn't even know where we were going.

ANTHONY: It sounds like a movie plot!

GARCIA: I understand there's a movie out called *The Dirty Dozen* that is patterned after this operation, but there were twenty-six of us on this mission. After the training we were put on a submarine and all twenty-six of us went to France. We emptied a certain building and destroyed all the high-ranking German officials who were there, including the women. They were having a party. We took every piece of paper that was in that building on every floor. We took maps and everything. I understand that mission was necessary for the planning of the Normandy invasion, and as a consequence I received a Presidential citation, and was commissioned lieutenant.

ANTHONY: And not one man was lost?

GARCIA: Not one man was even wounded!

ANTHONY: How many people did you destroy in that operation?

GARCIA: I'd say there were two hundred.

ANTHONY: You killed two hundred men?

GARCIA: Right.

ANTHONY: You said you were trained by a special Indian?

GARCIA: Well, karate and all that kind of thing has come to light by now. But this man was already using it at that time. He was a silent killer and an instant killer. He knew exactly what points to hit so you wouldn't even make a sound as you killed someone.

ANTHONY: He trained you?

GARCIA: Yes, he trained all twenty-six of us. He went along on the mission too.

ANTHONY: What about this thing with the bullet in his hand?

GARCIA: He had a fifty caliber bullet, he didn't have the machine gun, just the bullet. He walked up behind one of the sentries outside the building and stuck it in his eye. He just relaxed him and put him down on the ground very slowly without making a bit of sound. He killed a German shepherd dog there with a sock full of sand.

ANTHONY: This training you received was to kill. You were a lethal weapon; your body was a weapon. Did it just seem like second nature to you?

GARCIA: It was just an automatic, instantaneous thing.

ANTHONY: When you killed the policeman?

GARCIA: Yes. I wasn't going to shoot it out or anything. My intention was to take the gun out and put it on the sidewalk. But this policeman cocked his rifle and I thought I was shot, so I just started pumping.

ANTHONY: It was automatic because of your training?

GARCIA: Right. It is instilled in you, and you have to do it. When we came back from overseas Eleanor Roosevelt opened up a special rehabilitation camp, Camp Edwards in Massachusetts, and they put most of us there in that camp. But it didn't work, because we handcuffed the MPs to the post and took off for town. But those are the things that led up to my reacting automatically when certain movements were made against me.

ANTHONY: I heard you say one time that when you lost your wife there was no remorse and no tears shed, nothing took place in your life emotionally. But the moment you accepted Jesus as your Savior, that you humbled yourself and the tears flowed like water. Do you have total peace in your life tonight?

GARCIA: Definitely.

ANTHONY: How did it come to you?

GARCIA: By just opening my heart to Christ and accepting Him and knowing and believing His Word and standing upon His promises.

ANTHONY: Is the devil still working on you? Is he saying "Johnny, let's go get a fix; let's do this or let's do that?"

GARCIA: The devil is always going to be doing that, and more so with me, because I believe I was a general in the devil's army. But I feel much better being a private in Jesus' army!

ANTHONY: Religion is the quest for something. Jesus Christ is the answer. You've found Christ, and that is the answer; that is the key.

There's a little card out that says, "If you didn't like being born the first time, try being born again." That reminds me of what you've said this evening, Johnny. But I've done everything just as bad as what you've done; I just did it in a different way. And all of us do.

Here's a man who has killed a policeman, killed no telling how many hundreds in the war, received a Presidential citation for the killing, killed his cellmate in prison, was a heroin addict, lost his whole family, had nothing to live for, was sent to death row in San Quentin seven times, was strapped in the seat three times ready for the cyanide pellets to come down. And God, in His wisdom, has chosen him from among thousands of others to be His warrior today. He has given Johnny something beautiful; He's given him something called *a new life*.

Johnny Garcia, praise God for your life. You're going to get accolades; you're going to face flesh traps day after day after day. You're going to become a "trophy" for Christ. Ignore it all, and keep that innocence in Christ.

KYLE ROTE, JR.

Superstar of the Superstars! How would you feel to win over O. J. Simpson, Bob Seagren, Jean-Claude Killy, Stan Smith, and many others of the world in athletic competition? Kyle Rote, Jr. did, and became the Superstar of the Superstars! Kyle is a young man who grew up in the shadow of his father, Kyle Rote, Sr., a nationally-known celebrity in professional football. Unlike so many other celebrity kids, Kyle has grown up frank and open, clear-visioned, vital, refreshing, disciplined, who now says his professional soccer playing for the Dallas Tornados is his pulpit! "Open" is the most descriptive word that comes to mind in the several interviews done with Kyle Rote, Jr.

CHAPTER 10

KYLE ROTE, JR.

The Lord will not look for diplomas or awards or trophies;
He will look for scars!

ANTHONY: Our guest tonight is Kyle Rote, Jr., who is a superstar of the superstars in this country, and I guess in the world. During all the time he was on network television and was shown all over the world, he "walked the talk." He reflected Christ in his life. Kyle, what went through your mind when you knew you had won, and Howard Cosell was interviewing you?

ROTE: A number of people told me afterwards that they had never before seen a less jubilant winner. But to me the whole competition was a chance for me to share my own relationship with God. When we came to a climax in the competition, I was praying, just as I had tried to be in constant prayer throughout each of those days. But each day was a climax, too. Winning was a real point of contrast, because everyone was coming up and patting me on the back and saying, "Gee, Kyle, you did a great job!" And I was sitting there saying, "Gee, Lord, You did a great job!"

ANTHONY: One of the interesting things about being a Christian in this life is that we are, at the same time, Adam and Christ. There is the flesh, and there is the reality of Christ. You had to be awed a little bit to be with O. J. Simpson and other stars. What was your impression, meeting all those people?

ROTE: Well, as you say, awe at first, because they are held up so high in our society, almost to the point of worship. You never really know if they are human people. But you find out pretty quickly in talking to them that they are. While it was a great chance to get to see these guys, it was a greater chance to get to sit down and find out what is really going on with them and what makes them tick. Within that group of forty-eight superstars we had a wide, wide range of people.

ANTHONY: I understand there were quite a few born-again Christians in that group. But when it came to the time you realized you were in heads up competition with them, did you pray, "Lord let me win!"?

ROTE: No! I'll have to admit that I have been tempted in that direction. But all I can say is, "Lord, use me, and if it be in Your will, let me do the best I can, and whatever happens is great with me." I guess that's another reason why I wasn't as excited about winning as someone else might have been, because I knew I could just as easily have finished last. As long as the Lord's will was the result, I was content.

ANTHONY: I have one question, Kyle. Why didn't you run the obstacle race?

ROTE: Well, not to say that the good Lord couldn't get me over that wall, but it would have been pushing it!

ANTHONY: One of the biggest shocks I've ever had was when I went to your house after you had just won all that money. You and your wife live in an $85 a month apartment, and I just couldn't believe it. Compared to the homes of all those other people who were in the superstar competition with you, it was quite a contrast. What about your lifestyle? Has it changed, or is it going to change?

ROTE: Well, it has changed in the sense that so many more people are calling now, and we have the opportunity to share with a lot more people. I am just praying it doesn't change my outlook on life, and that my relationship with the Lord doesn't degenerate, because there is a lot of temptation in living, and there is a lot of temptation in fame. I can certainly think of times within the last week when I probably was exposed to both those temptations. It just helps me and Mary Lynne to keep aware of our priorities. We may have to move out of our apartment, but I think it is important that our lifestyle reflect the way we really feel. You mentioned what John Niland said about "walking the talk." I don't know that we could do that in a penthouse.

ANTHONY: Do you see any dangers now of becoming what people call "a trophy for Christ?" We in the flesh tend to make people trophies, but does Christ see any of us as trophies?

ROTE: I don't think He does. Each of us has his own place that God is directing us toward. There are people who in their day-to-day duties do His will more consistently than I do, or let Him direct their lives more consistently than I do. If there were any trophies to go out—not to say that there are—they would go to those people, not to me. You can't measure what would be a trophy for the Lord by what our society holds up as a trophy.

ANTHONY: Somebody said that when we finally stand before the Lord He is not going to look for our diplomas or our awards or our trophies; He's going to look for scars.

ROTE: Well, as I have always said, I just hope that on that day He recognizes me and what I've done for Him as easily as a lot of the kids recognize me for being the superstar. That's really the only prayer I can make.

ANTHONY: You are attending seminary now?

ROTE: Yes, I am.

ANTHONY: What is the purpose of your study? Do you feel the Lord is moving you toward becoming a preacher?

ROTE: In the last year I've begun to realize that a preacher's ministry is no more important in God's eyes than the ministry of a layman. A number of years ago I was drawn to thinking about entering the ministry because I saw it as the one way I could say, "Yes, I love You." Then I backed off, but now I feel that this is an area He wants me to go into. I cannot predict where He will lead me, but I think it will be tied in with kids and young people.

ANTHONY: I can just imagine someone in the audience saying, "Well, that's easy for Kyle to say about living the life, because now he's got security and he's a big superstar. But what about me? I've got a thousand dollars due on my house payment and I'm out of a job!" What would you say to that? A couple of months ago you were living on $1,400 a year, but now you're in a different situation.

ROTE: I think you know I was saying the same thing then.

ANTHONY: But that is one of the problems of fame. You close the door on people relating to you.

ROTE: That is part of what has been my effort in the last two or three years, to try to get people to realize that the big sports figures are human. I really don't know how to get at that.

ANTHONY: How did Howard Cosell take you? You could see the shock on his face after he interviewed you the first time.

ROTE: Someone said that after the first day of competition Howard was speechless. That's a miracle in itself! I guess the thing that surprised him was my attitude, contrasted with the attitudes of the other athletes in that group.

ANTHONY: Did you witness directly?

ROTE: Not to Howard, but I witnessed to many

others, mainly the kids and local residents there. I was very fortunate to be able to preach at the local church and have an opportunity to witness. I felt a well-rounded participation there, and I think the people felt that way too, because they didn't seem to be coming in just for the money.

ANTHONY: You have been on the program twice before and nobody knew you from Adam then, except for a few soccer nuts. But now we have a lot of new listeners tuned in because they've seen the publicity about you in the secular press, and they're listening now because you're a superstar. I don't know how to feel about that. That somehow doesn't seem right. Do you know what I mean?

ROTE: It isn't right that people in sports have that much power. But you have to realize that it does exist, and try to do the best you can with it.

ANTHONY: Kyle, you came to the Lord while relatively young. How did that happen?

ROTE: It goes back several months before the actual experience. I had done very well in sports and was well-off materially. I had a status that most people would look up to as the ultimate goal one could reach in society. But I found out after a great athletic victory, which seemed at that time to be the ultimate, that there had to be something more. No one had told me that kind of empty feeling after a victory even existed. Of course, I had been going to church very dutifully every Sunday with an Episcopal family, but not really knowing the peace and calm that comes about by having the Lord direct your life. I had participated in "Young Life" while I was in high school. I went to it for several reasons: to get into the social scene, and to meet a bunch of good-looking girls. It was kind of a status thing, and I enjoyed the meetings and the singing. I had the opportunity one summer to go to Colorado Springs to a Young Life camp. A camp like that can be a lot of fun with a lot of sharing and a lot of gospel message. I sat through several days of that thinking, "Well, I'm just putting up with this heavy stuff to do the fun stuff." I would attend the meetings at night so I could play volleyball with the whole group the next day.

Then I was sent out by myself on the side of a mountain. No one was with me, and I was just walking along and began to realize that I was really missing something. After sundown it got kind of scary. The thought of being alone can scare you. But I just said, "Hey, Lord, I've been in church all my life, but if You're there and there is something special You have for me, let me know about it." Then I thought, "Gee, that was nuts for me to say that." Though I felt sincere, I didn't realize the implications of what I'd said. But I did the same thing again the next night, and the Lord just took hold of me. It wasn't a violent, emotional sort of thing; I'm not an emotional type of guy. But there is no question that the impact was just amazing. I realized then how self-centered I was, and what a waste my life had been. I asked Jesus not only to come into my life, but to give me strength and direction to use the abilities He had blessed me with. If you could multiply a hundredfold the tremendous feelings of facing a challenge and then reaching it, that still would not equal the feeling one has when Jesus Christ is the center of his life and is directing his life.

ANTHONY: The grace of God is really beyond our explanation, isn't it?

ROTE: I was reading recently in Proverbs that you can't lean on your own understanding; you have to trust in the Lord with all your heart.

ANTHONY: But we still try to do both, don't we? Every day we try to lean on the old man.

ROTE: Or we try to lean on a college degree, and try to intellectualize the whole thing.

ANTHONY: The Bible says anything outside of faith is sin. I heard a speaker say once that a great shock for him was when he had gotten to know some of the greatest leaders all over the world, and he found out they didn't know any more than he did. That really sent him to the Bible. The same thing must have happened to you. You've met all your heroes now. Were any of these people you competed against your heroes a couple of years ago?

ROTE: Certainly Pete Rose was, and Jean-Claude Killy, the skier.

ANTHONY: Did he make the finals?

ROTE: No, he did not, but he was ill during semifinals. I guess we all sometimes dream about being an O. J. Simpson.

ANTHONY: You played O.J. in tennis.

ROTE: Yes.

ANTHONY: I saw that match; it was rough.

ROTE: It was. The last time I was here Ken Cooper was on with us, and he talked about being rookie of the year in the last soccer season. I've always considered that to be a real miracle. Now you talk about superstars, and it just blows my mind.

ANTHONY: What do you think when someone calls you "superstar?"

ROTE: It's a misnomer, no question. The whole superstar program is a child of television and the promotional market.

ANTHONY: You sell a lot of 3-M copiers! I heard you just signed a contract with them. Next year instead of Bob Seagren out there making all those copies, we'll see Kyle Rote, Jr., making all those copies.

Kyle, one of the biggest problems today is family relationships. The percentage of how many marriages end in divorce is incredible. I saw a statistic that among those who consider themselves to be born-again Christians, there is only one divorce out of almost every one-thousand, three-hundred marriages. What has your wife's presence meant to you in this whole thing?

ROTE: Well, when we were first married, and even before we were married, it was important to both of us to know that we each had our own continuing and developing relationship with the Lord. One of the pleasures of being married, which we began to discover just before we were married, is that we can incorporate our relationship with the Lord into something that matures us. Without that kind of basis for our relationship it would be tough for her to live with me, because I'm into a lot of things that put her under pressure.

ANTHONY: I think I just heard her say, "Amen!" Someone has said that in marriage if you look only at each other it will get boring after awhile. But if you both are looking at the Lord, it will never get boring; it will be constant growth.

Kyle, what do you consider to be one of the greatest needs of young people today?

ROTE: In my generation one of the great tragedies I see is that you can always have the radio on, you can always have the TV on, you can always be confronted with the media. People never want to be alone. I find this tendency in myself, but I value more than any time my quiet times when I can be alone and get a personal talk going with the Lord. Then you can sit down and shut out the rest of the world, shut off the radio, and shut out the neighbor next door. I think a lot of people miss that. They're never confronted with what they really are.

ANTHONY: In your private time with the Lord, what is He doing with Kyle Rote right now?

ROTE: Recently there has been a problem I've never had before. I say, "Lord, let me do Your work." So in the next day's mail come twenty-five invitations to go speak somewhere, and the following day the same thing happens. There is no question but there could be a luncheon and dinner engagement for me every day of the week. It comes down to this: are we looking right now at what good the Lord would like to do through me, or do I also need to be concerned about my own continued growth? If I stop my own personal growth, I'm going to be a disaster, and that is the inner conflict. Which invitations do I say "yes" to, and how do I know when to say "no?"

ANTHONY: The obvious thing is to say, "Pray about it." But let's be realistic. Every day you're getting twenty-five letters asking you to speak at a banquet somewhere, or go somewhere, or endorse this product, or whatever. What do you do? How do you know you're in the will of the Lord?

ROTE: Well, this is one of the problems Mary Lynne and I go through. A number of people have suggested setting a quota. I could say I am going to do four or five each week, and the first five that come along, I will do. I'm beginning to think that is the only way to do it.

ANTHONY: You want to hear another way? A person I'm acquainted with charges three or four thousand dollars for an appearance. That sort of gets it down!

ROTE: Yes, but . . . . I wouldn't judge your friend, whoever he is, but to me it is just as important to go to a Boy Scout group as it is to speak at the national convention of the Borden Milk Company. Maybe I'm way off base, but numbers are not a real part of the decision-making process.

ANTHONY: Did you get to fellowship much with Stan Smith and Roger Staubach at the superstar competition?

ROTE: Yes, more than any other situation would have allowed. All the people were from so many diverse sports, it was really unusual. I would never get a chance to visit with Stan Smith for two days under any other circumstances. Most conversations never got down to real Christian sharing—not because there wasn't a desire to do that, but because time interfered, and there were so many people around all the time wanting autographs. But it was great to see them. I would see a guy like Stan or Roger talking to a young kid, just as I would be talking to a young kid, but we could look across at each other and say, "Hey, praise the Lord! This is great!"

ANTHONY: You were talking about soccer being a witnessing opportunity that is unmatched in the other sports, because soccer is not "the sport" here in the United States. But in the rest of the world it certainly is.

ROTE: In over one hundred and forty countries around the world, soccer plays the same role football plays here in the United States. In fact, this is true in more countries than are members in the United Nations. For myself, and a number of other soccer players who are dedicated Christians and trying to learn to become more like Jesus, this could be a way for us to go out, using the mode of athletics, and have a ministry that could be unparalleled. When that might come about, I don't know; I'm just praying about it.

ANTHONY: Do you believe the Lord can speak to you? Do you hear His voice?

ROTE: I certainly do.

ANTHONY: What would you do if He said tomorrow, "Give up soccer."

ROTE: I'd do it. My wife knows that. That's part of surrendering our lives into the Lord's hands. We've talked about Ken Cooper, another one of our players, and he would feel the same way. Certainly if that were to happen I couldn't foresee how I would be taken care of materially. But that's part of taking that leap of faith.

ANTHONY: You have said you would like to play soccer a while longer, and you also said you felt you were called to the ministry. How do you relate those two?

ROTE: Well, ministry can be playing soccer. I wouldn't be playing the game otherwise. Being a superstar is, to me, the same sort of thing. At this time in my life I feel the Lord wants me to continue my studies toward the priesthood, and yet at the same time maintain my ministry in the vocation of soccer or superstar or sportsman.

ANTHONY: They are not necessarily mutually exclusive, are they?

ROTE: Not by any means. Some sports people may think that the sporting side of their lives has nothing to do with the rest of their lives. You think about people who are as intent about sports as Coach Lombardi used to be, or Tom Landry or Roger Staubach, and yet they never totally get away from what is most important in their life, no matter how hot it gets.

ANTHONY: Obviously there is a discipline that is required to do well in any sporting activity. There is also a discipline required in Christ. How do you see this? I know it is important for us. It seems to me the discipline that has been part of your life must be very helpful in serving Christ, because it's part of you.

ROTE: Yes, each thing feeds the other. If I were going to classify myself as being disciplined or undisciplined, I would also say I am undisciplined. But I have no doubt that discipline is required to meet the will of God, to meet what is His purpose for you.

ANTHONY: There is a discipline required in yielding.

ROTE: That's right.

ANTHONY: We tend to just yield whenever we happen to feel like it, but that is not what He wants us to do.

ROTE: We only yield in times of need.

ANTHONY: If we're drowning we yell, "Help! Here I am, Lord." But we have to have the discipline to yield all the time, and that is difficult.

What about your father? Kyle Rote, Sr., was all-everything in football here at SMU and the NFL, and you were growing up in that environment with him as a superstar. Did that kind of life bother you as a child?

ROTE: I think any time I see sports as an end in itself it bothers me. That is not to say my father's involvement in sports was with that feeling or that intent. But I have seen more tragedies occur because people have thought, "Well, making it to be all-American, or to be all-state, or to be all pro, that's the zenith of my life." To see them the first five minutes after they reach that goal, if they reached it, you could have nothing but pity and just pray for them. I keep thinking back to Tom Landry, and this was his feeling, too. In 1956 when they were playing the world championship, he said, "Hey, I've spent the last twenty-seven years of my life for this goal. Now that I've got it, I have nothing to live for."

ANTHONY: Did you feel any kind of an emotional letdown after the superstar competition was over?

ROTE: I was tired, but I probably felt a much greater letdown after I was named all-state football player, or after I was named most valuable player in the soccer league. To me it is an indication of hope that maybe I am growing. I was just so happy that when I said, "Lord, take over," in this whole superstar thing, He said, "Okay." He took me through it.

ANTHONY: Did you have any inkling beforehand, down deep inside, that you would win it? When you stopped and looked at Stan Smith, Bob Seagren, Jean-Claude Killy, O.J. Simpson, what did you think?

ROTE: No one has ever asked me that question before, but I'm a great believer that with God all things are possible, so I wasn't leaving out the possibility of finishing last or finishing first. I sometimes catch myself saying when I'm in preparation, "I know I want to win this thing, and I know if the Lord's with me, I can. So Lord, come and take over!" Then it goes right back to the whole selfish thing again.

ANTHONY: It's like praying, "Lord, help me kill my

enemies, or let's kill a commie for Christ." Of course, before it was over you knew you were winning, except that Bob Seagren was breathing down your neck. But what was the most exciting moment of that superstar competition?

ROTE: Well, this may sound corny, but the most exciting thing for me was to sit down with a group of young kids afterward and say, "It's nice to be here in your city, and it's nice to be participating in the superstars, but you know what I think is really important?" And their eyes lit up and they asked, "What?" I guess they thought I was going to say, "To meet O.J. Simpson," or something like that. Then I said, "To know that the Lord is directing my life." And that type of sharing, for me, was what the whole superstar thing was all about. I was hoping that was what the Lord would do with it. I could have gone out there three days prior to winning and said the same thing to the same group of kids, and they wouldn't have cared who I was. But now that I was a superstar and said something like that, they might go home to mom and want to know what I'm talking about.

ANTHONY: Your heart is obviously turned toward young kids, isn't it?

ROTE: Yes. I think there are so many pressures on them, especially in sports, to get away from what I think is the most important thing in life—knowing Jesus Christ. I don't think there is any other occupation that glorifies its people more than sports does, and it can be tragic to think that the only way to make your life worthwhile is to be quarterback for the Cowboys or center forward for the Tornados. What really counts is making Christ the Lord of your life.

SHIRA LINDSAY

Shira is an anomaly. Raised in a Christian family in Dallas, she is a born-again, Spirit-filled Christian who in 1967 moved to Israel, became an Israeli citizen, and converted to orthodox Jewry. A jump of that magnitude is too great for many people to comprehend, yet she explains the significance of her faith and actions with perception and conviction. Author, producer of films, a thorn in the side of many people, she is a beautiful girl who is not always understood when she speaks of her completed Judaism, and who has a message for all.

CHAPTER 11

SHIRA LINDSAY

Jesus isn't King of the Christians; He is King of the Jews.

ANTHONY: One of the Jewish leaders in America recently made a comment concerning the witnessing efforts that are being directed toward the Jewish people, both here and in Israel. He said, "If I had the world's greatest violin and I wanted to teach you how to play it, I wouldn't beat you over the head with it. I would play it." More on that later.

Our guest is Shira Lindsay, who has become well-known for her activities in Israel. Shira, we really don't know enough about what is happening in the Middle East. We realize that somehow, someway, what happens in Israel is important in the plan of God. But we don't really know what is happening. Tell us about your life in Israel.

LINDSAY: I would think that born-again believers know as much about what is going on in Israel as any Israeli knows. Actually, nobody knows what is going on, because there is no rhyme nor reason to what happens much of the time. No one can really say when or if a war is going to take place. Many times during the six years I've been in Israel I've had a visitor come and say, "There's going to be a war right away." I ask, "How do you know?" And they say, "Sadat, or Khadafy or somebody from the Arab countries has said that next month they're going to have war." Well, these rulers have been saying this every month since the Six Day War. So nobody knows. Even the Israel defense minister never takes these threats for granted. That is why the Israeli army is always on alert, because nobody knows what is going to happen. So don't feel badly if here in the U.S. some of us don't understand exactly what is going on. Nobody does except the Lord.

ANTHONY: How in the world did a pretty young girl from Dallas get strung out in Israel? You've been living there now since 1967.

LINDSAY: I went over there after the Six Day War to work on a documentary film on prophecy, the Scriptures, and what they say about Israel today, to see if it is true. I worked on this film for about a year. It is called *Dry Bones*. I had a number of different jobs besides the film work. By the time I finished I had fallen in love with Israel.

I was working at one time for a Jewish Agency writing articles for American Jewry to help keep their interest in Israel. One day my boss said to me, "Why are you, a Gentile girl, working for the Jewish Agency to write articles like this?" I said, "Well, so many people have done so many things against Israel for the last couple of thousand years, I just feel I want to do something—whatever I can—for Israel."

Then I began to talk to him and tell him how I know that according to the Scriptures God is going to be with Israel, and that my Messiah, whom I so believe in, is coming back to reign in Israel. I was so excited about it as I continued to talk to him that he said, "Well, if this is all true, if you really believe in the future of Israel like you say you do, why don't you become one of us?"

That was a possibility I had not even dreamed of, but that was the beginning of my long process of becoming an Israeli.

ANTHONY: Are you an Israeli citizen?

LINDSAY: Yes, I am.

ANTHONY: But you're not a Jew.

LINDSAY: I am a Jew.

ANTHONY: There is a Scripture which says, "For he is not a Jew who is one outwardly; neither is circumcision that which is outward in the flesh. But he is a Jew who is one inwardly; and circumcision is that which is of the heart, by the Spirit, not by the letter; and his praise is not from men, but from God" (Romans 2:28, 29).

LINDSAY: I became a Jew under their orthodox method. I am legally a Jew.

ANTHONY: Are you a fulfilled Jew?

LINDSAY: I am definitely a fulfilled Jew! The Lord fulfills everything I could possibly dream of. Life is just too exciting. You don't know what is coming next.

ANTHONY: Is your religion Judaism?

LINDSAY: Yes.

ANTHONY: What does that mean to you?

LINDSAY: Well, you see, Christians for many, many years have thought of Jews as non-believers. But if you go back to the Bible to the original faith that God gave to the Jews, it was a true faith He gave them. The Old Testament consists of three basic national covenants: the Abrahamic Covenant, which God has never revoked; the Mosaic Covenant, which the Jews themselves broke; and the New Covenant, which Jeremiah and all the other prophets promised. The Old Testament promises a Messiah to come to give salvation; it promises eternal life. Everything you could possibly want is right there. In fact, Jesus said, "You search the Scriptures . . . it is these that bear witness of me" (John 5:39). The only right that Jesus ever proclaimed was that He is the Messiah because the Scriptures tell about Him.

But Judaism went into something else besides Biblical Judaism or born-again Judaism. It went into what we call talmudic or rabbinical or traditional Judaism.

We have to talk about born-again Christians, because we're trying to differentiate between born-again Christians and nominal Christians. The vast majority of people, if you ask them if they are a Christian, will say "yes." But that is all they know about it. They don't even know what they're talking about. So Jews, when they think of Christians, don't think of a born-again person. They think of the Gentile world, which consists of every Gentile who ever claimed any part of Christianity. That includes Spain, which killed Jews, it consists of crusaders—those were all Christians as far as the Jew is concerned. The Russian Orthodox Church in Russia started the word **pogrom**, the killing and murdering and raping of Jews. These were all nominal Christians. They bore the name Christian, they felt they were Christians, they said they were Christians, they had Christian churches. But that was nominal Christianity, because the vast majority of them did not know what it meant to be born again.

We can say that just as there are nominal Christians and born-again Christians, there are nominal Jews and there are born-again Jews. There is nothing wrong with being a Jew. God created the Jews and He has a great plan for them. But in order for them to find this plan, they must be reconciled to their God, the God of Abraham, Isaac and Jacob. And the **only** way the Scriptures give for a Jew to be reconciled to the God of Abraham, Isaac and Jacob is through the Messiah, Jesus.

ANTHONY: I asked you earlier whether you are a fulfilled Jew. We have talked to several people of the Jewish faith who were believers, but they didn't call themselves Christians; they called themselves fulfilled Jews.

LINDSAY: You see, the word "Christian" comes from Greek. Now that whole concept never originated with the Jews. The word "Christian" originated with the Gentiles, and it means **Messianic.** And the word "Christ" means **Messiah.** I would say eighty percent of Christians don't know what it means, and ninety-nine percent of the Jews do not know that "Christ" means **Messiah.**

Just as Spanish people say Jesu Cristo, and the Americans say in English "Jesus Christ" because their background is Gentile, we use **Yeshua Hamashiach**, Jesus the Messiah, which is definitely Hebrew. The whole concept originated with the revelation of God to the Jews.

ANTHONY: What about the some two hundred times in the New Testament which speak of a position—"in Christ," "in Him," and so forth. Is there any problem in that area with regard to what the fulfilled Jews do believe?

LINDSAY: I don't believe there is any problem at all. "In Christ" just means "in the Messiah."

ANTHONY: What does Messiah mean?

LINDSAY: Messiah means "The Anointed One." I have often thought about that name, Messiah. Of all the names the Savior could have been called—He could have been called Chief, or Great Man, or any number of things. But the Lord chose to magnify that name, Messiah, meaning "The Anointed One." The more I think about that, the more I realize that the anointing upon a person is the most important thing they could have to fulfill God's will. Every orthodox Jew knows that the Messiah is the one who is coming to save Israel. Whether he believes in Jesus or not, He knows the meaning of Messiah.

ANTHONY: If you're going to be anointed, you have to be anointed by someone. As the Messiah, He is still bringing glory to God. That's an interesting point I've never realized before.

LINDSAY: This whole thing of Jews who believe in Jesus actually started with Abraham. Abraham saw a person whom the Scripture calls God. Abraham saw Him with his own eyes. He walked like a man and Abraham gave Him food (Genesis 18). I've talked to orthodox people about this, and they are just stymied. How could Abraham talk to a person whom the Scripture calls God?

Jacob saw a man, whom he wrestled with, and he asked Him, "What is Your name?" (Genesis 32:29). And this man would not tell him. Yet Jacob turned around later and said, "I saw God face to face."

Joshua saw a man who identified himself as commander of the army of the Lord. Joshua bowed down and worshipped Him. Gideon saw this man, and Samson's parents saw this man. He came to them and they called Him the angel of the Lord. Now in Hebrew **angel** just means "messenger", someone sent. So the parents of Samson said to Him, "What is Your name?" And this person said, "Why do you ask My name, seeing it is wonderful?" (Judges 13:18). ("Wonderful" here means "incomprehensible.")

The Scripture says, "For a child will be born to us . . . And His name will be called Wonderful, Counselor . . . " (Isaiah 9:6). So this person has been working and saving Israel unknown times. And that continues right up until today.

ANTHONY: Historians say that from the very start of the good news, the gospel, there have been two major forces pulling within Christendom. On the one hand is the Judaic, legalistic influence, the holiness influence emphasizing that men are holy by what they do. On the other hand is the humanistic influence that man's basic purpose is to glorify man. Both of these forces have been struggling and tearing apart the strength and the power of the gospel, and we see that today.

How is the message of grace accepted by the fulfilled Jew? It seems so foreign to their way of thinking.

LINDSAY: Historians like to give names to everything and box them up and analyze them. But to me, these tendencies you are talking about are just human tendencies. I've known little churches in the back bushes of south Texas someplace that are the most legalistic type of people, and they've scarcely heard of the Jews. You see, human nature just tends to begin to substitute legalism for grace.

ANTHONY: Can you think why?

LINDSAY: Yes. God has given us the Holy Spirit to guide us in a very constructive way, moment by moment. This is the New Covenant. The New Covenant lives in our hearts. It is not a law written down on a piece of paper, it is a constructive thing and the Holy Spirit leads us moment by moment. Now when people start leaving this walk in the Spirit, they've got to have some really strong laws to keep themselves together. So laws begin to substitute for the presence of God, whether you are a Jew or a Gentile.

ANTHONY: We stand on the law and follow the rules and say, "Look at me, I'm humble."

LINDSAY: Every church and every synagogue has tradition. Now tradition with the Holy Spirit is all right. A service which takes place every Sunday morning at the same time is all right if the Spirit is there. But there may be a church that is deader than a doornail at 9:00 on Sunday morning, and someone could come along and say, "In this particular situation I think it would be better if we have a 2:00 service" and people would die. They've connected that 9:00 hour with holiness. It is human nature to do that.

ANTHONY: I didn't mean to impute all legalism to the Jews or to the Judaic influence, but my question still remains. How do the Jews accept grace?

LINDSAY: People, especially orthodox Jews, equate Judaism with one covenant, the Mosaic Covenant. And that is not the way God gave it at all. First He gave an Abrahamic Covenant. It was a faith covenant. It required nothing from the Jews. They had this covenant for over four-hundred years, and that is a long time. They lived under this covenant for four-hundred years before they had the Mosaic Covenant. Just think, the United States has been under a Constitution for less than two-hundred years, and we think that is really a long time.

So ask yourself, "Why did God come along four-hundred years later and give the Mosaic Covenant to the Jews?" The answer is in the Scriptures. The prophets said, "You Jews, you began to disobey God down in Egypt; you started worshipping idols." You know the golden calf at Sinai? The Jews didn't start thinking about a golden calf only when they got to the desert. They had begun to take on this idolatry down in Egypt.

Second, God had promised Israel to take them to the Promised Land. This was part of the Abrahamic Promise. So when Moses came along and said, "Now is the time to go," do you think the Jews were just waiting to go to the Promised Land? They said, "Who are you?" And Moses fled for his life.

So it goes to show that the people who were living under the beautiful faith covenant of Abraham did not keep his covenant. But what was worse, they didn't realize they were doing anything wrong. It was really hard for God to punish them, because they didn't even know they were doing anything wrong, because God had not asked anything of them.

The Scriptures tell that God gave this second covenant four-hundred years later simply to show them when they were doing right and when they were doing wrong. So God said, "Okay, Mosaic Covenant: number one, when you are doing good I will bless you, I will keep you. Number two, when you do wrong—and these are the things you have to do to do wrong—then I'm going to curse you." You read the 28th chapter of Deuteronomy if you want to see some terrible, terrible curses. This is part of the Mosaic law. Many times when I think of my beloved orthodox Jewish brothers and their great love for the Mosaic law—I realize that they don't know how terribly they are being cursed, because that is part of the Mosaic law.

The point is that the third covenant God gave was given because of His love for the Jewish people. He had promised to bless Israel through the Abrahamic Covenant. But because of the Mosaic Covenant they were receiving all these curses, which included being scattered to the ends of the earth. So the only thing God could do was to bring along a new covenant. And no Messiah could be a Messiah without a new covenant. You ask how the Jews got tied up in the law. The Mosaic Covenant was only the second of three covenants which God gave. We have to look at the whole system of faith that God gave to the Jews, not just one covenant.

ANTHONY: The Mosaic Covenant actually left them without excuse, didn't it?

LINDSAY: Yes, because it wrote out in black and white

what is sin.

ANTHONY: Without law there isn't sin.

LINDSAY: Right. This was to be a schoolteacher so they would have no excuse. That's why David could say, "There is no one who does good, not even one" (Psalm 14:3), because he had the law to show him that he couldn't be righteous.

ANTHONY: Paul said in Romans that sin was revealed by the law.

LINDSAY: Which is a marvelous thing. No person without God can receive salvation until he realizes he is a sinner. I resent very deeply people saying that God broke or ended the Mosaic law. He never did anything of the kind. It was Israel who broke that covenant. Jeremiah 31:31, 32 says, "Behold, days are coming, declares the Lord, when I will make a new covenant with the house of Israel and with the house of Judah, not like the covenant which I made with their fathers in the day I took them by the hand to bring them out of the land of Egypt, My covenant which they broke . . . " God doesn't go around breaking covenants; it was Israel which broke that covenant.

ANTHONY: That is a heavy covenant.

LINDSAY: It is a tremendous covenant. He said, "I will write my law upon your hearts." It means that we are not any more guided by laws that are written on tablets of stone.

ANTHONY: That is the Holy Spirit.

LINDSAY: It means that when a church gets to the place where they make one law after another, they are going back to the old law which was given before the Holy Spirit lived and dwelled in our hearts.

ANTHONY: In Jesus the law was fulfilled. A lot of people don't stop to think what that really means. This does away with any thought of destruction of the law. It was never destroyed. But it was completed and fulfilled in Jesus. And again, if we get positional and see we are in Him, that's where the fulfillment is. If you are not in Him there is no fulfilled law.

LINDSAY: I think the Mosaic law is beautiful; it was sent

from God. But we have to understand that when God gives a law like that, it must have punishment. Because a law without punishment is not law at all, it is just some suggestions. And God did not give the ten suggestions, He gave the Ten Commandments. So when we have these laws, that means that people must be punished if they break them. When Jesus fulfilled the law, He not only fulfilled the beautiful things by keeping the law; He also fulfilled these punishments, the penalty of the law.

ANTHONY: What about witnessing to an orthodox Jew?

LINDSAY: There is a way to do it and a way not to do it. The first thing is this: I would never try to convert a Jew into another religion. Religion never did anybody any good anyway. The only thing I have to offer is a witness of the person of God through Jesus.

ANTHONY: That brings me back to the statement we made at the beginning about proselytizing in the Jewish community. What he is saying is, "Live the life."

LINDSAY: We know there are people in the Presbyterian church, or the Lutheran church, or the Methodist church who are not truly born again. Everybody is aware of that. Nobody would say that every person in that church is born again. But let's say a Southern Baptist believer goes into a Presbyterian church and says, "For you to be saved you must come out of your church and join the Baptist Church." Or vice versa. Let's say an Episcopalian goes into any church and says, "You aren't saved, and in order for you to find God you must come over and join our Episcopal church." Or to the Catholics we might say, "For you to find the Lord you must now become a Protestant."

The point is, how many of these people would ever find the Lord? They would get so jammed up with thinking about leaving their church and leaving their friends, that Jesus would get lost in the dust.

I am against the idea of telling a Jew, "You no longer need to be a Jew; you should come over and join the Christian church." Now **that** is going to keep him from coming to the Lord. The only thing a Jew needs to do is to repent of his sins and believe in the salvation of God—and "salvation" in Hebrew is **Yeshua. Yeshua** is Hebrew for "Jesus". Yeshua is the personified salvation of God.

Not long ago I was in a Kathryn Kuhlman meeting and she asked how many people were present from various denominations she named. I felt like getting up and saying, "Why don't you ask how many Jews are here?" Jews have always been expected to melt into the background and fit into someone else's church, and then when the Jews, like the young "Jews for Jesus" or Messianic Jewish groups want to remain Jewish some people say, "Oh, you're building up the middle wall again!"

Well, no one says anything about the Presbyterians building up the wall, or the Methodists building up the wall. We are unified in the Spirit. A friend of mine who is a Jewish believer told me about an Italian pastor from Chicago who has an Italian church with services in Italian. He came up to her and said, "You have no right to have a Jewish group of believers." Yet he felt there was nothing wrong with his having an Italian group of believers! The Scripture says, "There is neither Jew nor Greek, . . . neither male nor female" (Galatians 3:28). That means that in the Spirit we are all one. Just as I am female and others are male in the body of Christ, there are Jews and there are Greeks. God made the Jews, and a Jew should be really proud of being a Jew, just like other people are proud of being whatever they are.

ANTHONY: You mentioned "building up the wall again." But the message of Christ is that there is nothing between. It must grieve God to see how we get so hung up on how we ought to worship. Most people probably think that you don't exist. You can't be a Jew and be a Christian; you've got to be one or the other. But the message is, "Let nothing deter you from the simplicity of Christ, the truth of oneness in the Spirit."

Christianity and Judaism do not conflict, except as men look at them. Christianity is an extension or fulfillment of

Judaism.

LINDSAY: I would go even further. There was a time of the Jews, and there is a time of the Gentiles. Now when God's center of operation left the Jewish people, His favor left them for a season and came over to the Gentiles. Because of this fact the Jewish people lost their center of attraction, and it went over into a very Gentile-Roman roots type of thing. But in Romans 11 Paul talks about the "holy root." If you study those Scriptures, he is talking about Abraham. He says, "If the root be holy, the branches are too" (Romans 11:16). Now this root is the Jews.

We as Gentiles (at least I used to be a Gentile) are brought into this original Jewish or Israeli root. So actually a Jew doesn't become a nominal Christian or Gentile. But a Gentile when he becomes a Christian is doing nothing less than becoming a spiritual Jew. In other words, the Jewish people are now his brothers. You will find that the people who are really stepping into spiritual things and are aware of what God is doing have a natural affinity for the Jewish people today.

ANTHONY: We actually becomes citizens of Israel.

LINDSAY: Yes.

ANTHONY: I have a friend who flies overseas a lot, and she says there is a tremendous difference between the New York Jew and the Israeli Jew. It's unbelievable. It's as if they are from two different worlds. Yet some of them who have left New York and have gone to Israel are caught up in that same spiritual oneness.

LINDSAY: Remember that the love of Jesus does not require reciprocation. We love the Jews because of all the marvelous things God has done through them and for them. I believe the Israeli Jew is freer of complexes because he is a free man and he is a part of a majority. Anytime you have a group of people who comprise a majority, they are usually freer of complexes. But those in a minority group have certain problems to overcome. This is true in any nation.

If you are an average American and you want to know

what this is like, go live in some other country and become a minority, and see the problems you will face. I don't think a person can ever really understand minority problems unless you've been there.

ANTHONY: What about the average citizen on the street in Israel? Even though they may be orthodox Jews in their religion, do they sense the hand of God in the daily life of their nation today, as we see it? It seems to me if I were a citizen there I would sense something supernatural. Do they?

LINDSAY: I would say as a whole, no. The reason being that in Israel the orthodox Jews are the only legal religious group. The only religion an Israeli can choose is orthodox Judaism. The majority of Israelis, if I am not mistaken, are atheists. All they have is orthodox Judaism or atheistic Judaism, and the point that I just love to shout from the housetops is, "Praise God, we now have an alternative! We have Biblical, Scriptural Judaism, the Judaism given by God!" We have this instead of talmudic Judaism which just says, "I am a Jew because I am a Jew because I am a Jew." Or the orthodox, traditional thing. What an alternative! I don't blame those atheists for being atheists. Now there are some marvelous orthodox people with whom I have wonderful rapport. But so many times orthodox Judaism does what every orthodox anything does—it makes you hate-filled anti-Semites. And any time we are hate-filled we are not expressing the love of God—I don't care whose book you write it in. For instance, the bomb that was put outside my house in Israel. It was most likely put there by a religious Jew. But you see, he was hate-filled.

ANTHONY: Hey, wait a minute! You can't just skim over that. When were you bombed? I guess I read about that in **Time** magazine. That kind of made you nervous, didn't it?

LINDSAY: Well, not really. The newspaper men and the radio and television men made me a lot more nervous than the bomb did. It was over in a flash.

ANTHONY: Did it go off?

LINDSAY: Yes.

ANTHONY: Was it loud?

LINDSAY: Very loud.

ANTHONY: Did you get hurt?

LINDSAY: Not a scratch! It was right outside my door in the hall, and it damaged the hall and knocked out the lights. I would say Satan meant it for evil, but God turned it into good.

ANTHONY: Were there any notes with it?

LINDSAY: No, but it was the beginning on the part of many Israelis of their being interested in Biblical Judaism. Always before, orthodox Jews could say to a person who was seeking God, "You can't talk about Jesus. He is not for you because He is for the Christians. He is not for the Jews." So the person wouldn't even consider Jesus, because they think He is for the Christians or the Gentiles, not for the Jews. Now there are these young Jewish believers who are very happy they are Jews. They have found **why** they are Jews, and in fact they are more interested in their Judaism and their background and history than ever before. They are saying, "We have found what it means to be a Jew." Now this has infuriated some of the orthodox because they no longer have this escape of saying Jesus is for the Christians. We are saying, "No, don't be a Christian; be a born-again Jew!"

ANTHONY: So that freaks them out a little bit.

LINDSAY: Yes, and another thing is this: orthodox Jews have been able to say to Biblical Jews: "You're a traitor to your people. You've turned your back on your people; you've gone and joined this church that has persecuted the Jews for thousands of years." Now the Jews are saying, when they find the Lord, "We didn't join any church; we just joined Jesus, the Savior, the King of the Jews."

ANTHONY: Do you feel a compulsion or a need to conform to Jewish customs?

LINDSAY: I take delight in keeping many of the customs of the Jews. I think Paul says clearly that Gentiles should not take on the law of the Jews for their salvation, because this has never been a part of their background. He said for those who are uncircumcised to remain uncircumcised, and vice versa. On the other hand, he took Timothy and circumcised him because of his witness to the Jews. I don't care whether a Jew keeps the law or not as long as he realizes this does not buy him righteousness with God.

What if a preacher came along in the States and said to those who come down to accept the Lord as Savior, "Now since you have found Jesus you can no longer keep any holidays which we have here in America. If you keep Thanksgiving, that's the end of you. You can't do that, because you're saved by faith. Don't keep Christmas anymore, because that's not even in the Bible." Pretty soon we would just think of that man as "that guy who doesn't believe in Thanksgiving or Christmas." It's part of a tradition. The point is, if someone thought by keeping Christmas they were good enough to get to heaven, that would be absurd. But it's different for something like Passover. We know **why** there is a Passover, we know why there is a Day of Atonement. And I just enjoy thoroughly being a part of all this beautiful tradition. I haven't substituted it for God; it just adds to my cultural identity with the Jewish people, whom I love.

ANTHONY: But there are some requirements God has made which are to born Jews or nationalist Jews who are of the blood line, that really do not apply to anybody else. These have nothing to do with an individual's salvation, but there are some requirements and commandments God has made to keep them as a separate people.

LINDSAY: Yes, absolutely. When Paul said, "You observe days and months and seasons and years" (Galatians 4:10), he was very furious about it because they were picking this up, although it had nothing to do with their background. It's like some missionary going to Africa and taking Thanksgiving over there and telling the native, "Now you've got to observe this."

They would connect that with righteousness somehow. On the other hand, Paul said, "Let no one act as your judge in regard to food or drink or in respect to a festival . . . or a Sabbath day" (Colossians 2:16). So as long as we keep righteousness and cultural identity separate, I think we are free.

Paul never told a Jew, "Don't keep the law." It's not good, neither is it bad. It might help someone find God, but it won't keep him away from God as long as he realizes that he cannot win righteousness through the law. That's the whole point.

ANTHONY: At Jesus' crucifixion the veil was rent from top to bottom and opened up the Holy of Holies, and then the Holy Spirit came at Pentecost. What about the ministry of the Holy Spirit? How is that accepted?

LINDSAY: You see, Jewish people coming into a born-again experience with the Lord have never been taught pros or cons, for or against the twentieth-century working of the Holy Spirit. So it is just as natural as falling off a log. A Jewish person may find Jesus as his Messiah and receive an infilling of the Holy Spirit at the same time, because he is making this great leap into a knowledge of the personal God. He expects God to work supernaturally; he doesn't expect this to be another set of traditions or religious rules. It is no problem with Jewish people.

JW LUMAN

When you see JW, he looks like he just stepped out of the chutes at a professional rodeo. He is as adept at rounding up cattle on the open range as he is proficient in teaching the Bible. A dynamic, magnetic young man who began preaching when he was fourteen years old, he lives the life of Christ twenty-four hours a day. This interview may shock you, may change cherished opinions, but listen to a man who truly lives the life.

CHAPTER 12

JW LUMAN

Sharing Christ is not sitting around talking about Jesus—it is giving your life twenty-four hours a day.

ANTHONY: Over the past two or three years, I have had the privilege of interviewing many hundreds of people on radio and television. I have talked to most of the Christian superstars and trophies for Christ. Many people have asked me who was the most outstanding or who was the best teacher. Our guest tonight is the best. He is someone most people have never heard of, but he is the best teacher I have ever met. I feel privileged to also call him a good friend. Our guest is JW Luman, director of Boys' Valley Ranch.

Jesus was talking to His disciples at one point and He said, "Unto you it is given to know the mystery of the kingdom of God" (Mark 4:11). I wonder if He was talking about us too? I wonder what the mystery of the kingdom of God is? I wonder what depth of understanding it would take to know the kingdom of God? I wonder if any of us ever really begins to know, or are we just seeing through a glass darkly? We come up with so many opinions about so many things; I wonder what God thinks about our opinions? Unto us it is given to know the mystery of the kingdom of God. JW, what does that mean?

LUMAN: It must have to do with the plan the Father has for His sons, since the Scripture mentions "the hidden wisdom, which God ordained before the world" (1 Corinthians 2:7). "The mystery which hath been hid from ages and from generations, but now is made manifest to his saints" (Colossians 1:26). I think that mystery actually is the life of Christ, which must be revealed to and in every believer before they can begin to please the Father and enter into the fullness of His life. I think each time the word "mystery" is used in the Scriptures it points toward that life which is Christ. The glory and fullness and revelation of that mystery is that God revealed to us that we are in Christ, and He reveals Christ in us so we might by that knowledge and faith begin to be motivated by and actually live the very life that **is** Christ.

ANTHONY: That we might be called the children of God? John said, "Behold, what manner of love the Father hath bestowed upon us, that we should be called the sons of God" (1 John 3:1). Love. That is the Key.

What happens if someone is listening who says, "That sounds great. I'd love to know what they're talking about, but I don't feel the need to know." I just had someone say that to me. It sounds contradictory. They said, "I'm happy for you that you have found God, and He has found you, but I just don't feel the need to know that." What do you say to someone like that? Do you say anything?

LUMAN: I don't know. I think coming to Christ is brought about by spiritual hunger, which is often the result of a real crisis in a person's life. It's a shame, but many people have to wait until they fall into a crisis before they see a real need for knowing Christ, or a need for knowing anything outside themselves. They wait until everything else falls apart.

ANTHONY: Do you think we use this mystery for our own purposes? It seems to me the mystery of the Son of God is that everything has to be self-giving. We talk a lot about how that mystery can bless me, or what it can do for me. What do you think about all that?

LUMAN: 1 John 3:1, 2 says: "Behold, what manner of love the Father hath bestowed upon us, that we should be called the sons of God . . . Beloved, now are we the sons of God, and it doth not yet appear what we shall be: . . . " This is the mystery. " . . . But we know that, when He shall appear, we shall be like Him; . . . " This is the hope of the mystery. ". . . for we shall see Him as He is." And this is the revelation of the mystery. The third verse says: "Every man who has this hope (or this knowledge or this assurance) in him, purifieth himself, even as He is pure." This means the knowledge of this mystery causes us to live as Christ, to live daily the very life of Christ. The mystery of godliness which God reveals to us in Christ has nothing to do with us, but has everything in the world to do with living the one life which is Christ Jesus, and the entering into the fullness of that life.

Recently, I have become aware of the fact that there is but one life. And yet to live that life costs us everything.

ANTHONY: It must be the total giving up, the total denying of self, following Him and abiding in Him, in His life. That's where the life is; that is when the Father is well pleased.

LUMAN: You know, His life is a mystery to the natural mind. Paul speaks of this mystery so many times. Anything having to do with the life of Christ is a mystery to the natural mind and cannot be understood by it. If we could figure it out it would no longer be a mystery. Instead we try to figure out how we can turn it to our advantage. The Father has started everything that He might have sons, and He has revealed to us the great, mysterious way in which He will have sons. And the way is that He has placed every believer in Christ, and therefore it is absolutely necessary that all those whom He has placed in Christ come to the knowledge of His life and begin to be motivated by His life. We must come to the knowledge of the mystery of God, the thing that God has done to enable Him to have sons. He has placed us in Christ and placed His Son in us. By the revelation of His Son in us, He teaches us that there is but one life that pleases Him, and that there is but one life He strives to have in every believer. That life, and the revelation of that life, is the mystery of God and the mystery of godliness.

ANTHONY: Someone said there are two things God can't do: He can't lie, and He can't create sons. It points up to the fact that this is the whole purpose of salvation: sonship and fellowship.

LUMAN: Paul says, ". . . that I should preach . . . the unsearchable riches of Christ; And to make all men see what is the fellowship of the mystery . . . " (Ephesians 3:8, 9). There is a fellowship among those to whom the mystery has been revealed. And I stress again, this mystery is that life we have in Christ. It is the means and the message and the fullness by which God achieves that which He desires—sons. Oh, if we could only see that the only life that pleases Him is Christ's, not that which we call Christ, or think is Christ-like, but **Christ Himself**. He isn't after a lot of little imitation Jesuses running around on this earth; He is only pleased with the one life of His Son. That is the mystery of it, and yet God reveals that life. He reveals that mystery **in** every believer who will search for the truth.

ANTHONY: The grace of God is that we have been allowed to become partakers of this salvation of Christ. I sometimes think we put the wrong emphasis on it when we say, "God saved me," or, "I am saved." Am I wrong to think that way?

LUMAN: No, that's very true. The carnal religion puts the total emphasis upon the believer rather than upon the life the believer receives, which is Christ.

ANTHONY: Hebrews 3:14 says, "We are made partakers of Christ." That's where the life is; that's where the dying seed must come into play.

What is the mystery of the blood? How can the blood of Christ cleanse us? I know it does. I claim it; I accept it; I confess it. We overcome Satan by the blood of Christ and the word of our testimony. But I don't understand it. Does anybody understand the mystery of the blood?

LUMAN: I don't think anyone understands it fully. In

Romans 5 it speaks of the blood. I call this the "much more" chapter. It talks about the sin of one man, but "much more" we have received the life of another man. Keep in mind that Romans 5 is talking about Adam and Christ. It says that though we are all dead and though we are all sinners in Adam, "much more" (not just to the same degree) "they which receive abundance of grace . . . shall reign in life by one, Jesus Christ" (Romans 5:17). Most believers think when they are saved they are restored Adamites. But the Scriptures don't teach that. They think, "Now we have restored dominion." But it is so much more than that. Adam lost more than the power over a tiger or a lion; the Scripture says Adam was put out of "the way of the tree of life" (Genesis 3:24). The first believers were called "people of the way." Jesus said "I am the way." Adam lost the way. But we got much more than Adam lost.

Romans 5:9 says, "Much more, then, being now justified by His blood, we shall be saved from wrath through Him." There is a mystery of the blood, and I think it is wonderful. God demanded the shedding of blood. The law demanded the shedding of blood. And the mystery wrapped up in the blood is the fact that Christ, by shedding His blood, fulfilled the law and the just demands of God. We, by what He did, were then justified by His blood. But salvation is much more than justification.

There is more than that. "We shall be saved from wrath through Him. For if, when we were enemies, we were reconciled to God by the death of His Son, much more, being reconciled, we shall be saved by His life. We also joy in God through our Lord Jesus Christ by whom we have now received the atonement," or "at-one-ment" with God (Romans 5:9-11). I could never figure out how I was covered by the blood until I began to see that in this Scripture the blood brings justification. It satisfies the righteous demands of God.

ANTHONY: Not that our flesh and blood is made perfect.

LUMAN: No, we shall be saved through Him, through His life. It points to the fact that just because a person has come and said, "I believe on Jesus," that is not enough. And just because Jesus has died on the cross and shed His blood, that is not enough. Unless you live His life, that won't do you anymore good than if I killed an alley cat and threw it in the freeway in your name. It is the living of His life. The mystery of the blood is that it justifies us; it enables us to live; it clears the slate. That's part of God's mystery. It had to be done to justify us. But it is the living of His life by which we shall be saved.

ANTHONY: That is not a message people like to hear.

LUMAN: Well, they didn't like it when Jesus said, "I am the way, the truth, and the life" either. He wasn't declaring a historical truth; He was telling them, "What you are doing is not good enough. I am the way."

ANTHONY: All the Jewish laws, and the ten commandments which were so strict, nobody ever lived by them that I know of. Maybe somebody did. But Jesus came along and said, "You not only have to live by them; you can't even think about not living by them."

Okay, then what do we do? Because I think about a lot of things. The answer is, you enter into the door by faith, by the vehicle of the blood, and then partake of the flesh. The only thing you can conclude from all this is that we need Him.

LUMAN: That is right. It is His life. There is only one life that pleases God, and it's to live His life. If we cease living that life, nothing works. You either live that life totally, or you totally regress.

ANTHONY: JW, when we talk about things which are very "you-directed," such as, "By His stripes ye are healed," or "God shall supply all your needs" the phones ring off the wall with people claiming promises and Scriptures for their needs. When we talk like we are tonight, simply uplifting Christ, the phones are silent. I wonder why?

LUMAN: I think of the multitudes who followed Jesus,

and He only had twelve disciples. The disciples sat at His feet and listened to His words, and the multitudes cried out for the healing. There is no place mentioned in the Bible where Jesus ever healed a disciple. He never healed a disciple. They were the ones who, after the Lord sent the Holy Spirit at Pentecost, proclaimed the life of Christ. They worked the miracles of Christ, but they proclaimed the life of Christ. They did not proclaim the miracles; they proclaimed the life and worked the miracles. I am all for miracles and healings and all those things He does, but to emphasize those things and not proclaim His life, in my humble opinion, is apostasy.

ANTHONY: You say some interesting things!

LUMAN: I'm just saying that I believe in what the Lord does, but I believe so much stronger in the Lord. And I think the apostles were the same way. They certainly did not follow Jesus for the healing, because He didn't heal any of them. He just shared His life with them.

ANTHONY: I wonder if that is what Jesus was talking about in Matthew 7:21 and 22, "Not every one that saith unto me, Lord, Lord, shall enter into the kingdom of heaven; but he that doeth the will of my Father which is in heaven." But people are not consciously committing apostasy. How do those who are honestly seeking and searching find the mysteries that need to be shared?

LUMAN: The key is the word "honestly" seeking and searching. A person desiring to be healed is not committing anything wrong; he is just making his need known to the Lord. But we've got a lot of people making a gospel out of getting healed. The Scriptures say, how shall they believe except they hear, and how shall they hear except somebody be sent? (Romans 10:14, 15). I believe the answer is that those who know the true gospel preach it, proclaim it, teach it, and share it. For a believer who is truly born again, the depth of his soul cries out for the satisfaction of the life of Christ, and that goes so far beyond the physical ailments or needs. Some people think the only time they are ever touched by God is when they get healed; but there is a far greater touch, and that is the touch of the very life of Christ. I have been healed many, many times, but there came a point when I came to the knowledge of the life within when my life was changed.

ANTHONY: It wasn't changed; it was exchanged!

LUMAN: Well, a great difference was made. You enter into His life. There is a great deal of difference between one who enters into His life, and one who just follows after the things Jesus does. The difference is so clear in the Scripture: those who followed for the loaves and the fishes, and those who stood there and broke the loaves and the fishes and supplied the need. There is a lot of difference between those who sit down and eat and those who hand out the food.

You know, Ole, I like to think the reason the phones don't ring when we talk about the Lord like this is because people are responding to that life we are sharing. That's not something you call up on the telephone for; that is a fellowship you search for. Many times that is probably the reason it gets rather quiet. When I go somewhere and teach this in a class, the only thing I hear is the rustling of Bible pages, because people are searching the Scriptures. For the first time we are not talking about something that centers around ourselves; we're talking about something that centers around the Lord. We just sit there and eat.

ANTHONY: We go back to the idea that you enter in at the door, and eat the lamb.

LUMAN: You talk very little when you eat; your mouth is too full.

ANTHONY: JW, in your own words, what is the message of sonship?

LUMAN: The message of sonship is the Father's message to the believer. That message is found in the knowledge of the Son of God, Christ Himself. There came a time in my life, after having served the Lord for a lot of years, and after having preached for a long time, when the Lord began to deal with me concerning **His** message, His gospel. What is God trying to say? We have politicians throughout the country today who have something to say in trying to get their point across, passing their legislation, and so forth. We have preachers who take the pulpit every Sunday morning and they all have something to say. They strike out against this or strike out against that. The people in the news media have their stories to tell. We have singers who sing, not necessarily for entertainment, but because they too have something to say, and they're trying to get their message across.

God has something to say. "In the beginning was the Word, and the Word was with God, and the Word was God" (John 1:1). Now God's message comes from the beginning. It doesn't center around me, because I'm not from the beginning. It doesn't center around you, because you are not from the beginning. It centers around what God wants, and that is **sons.** That is what he wants. He has a message which declares the very intent of His heart. His message is not salvation; that is a means to sonship. His message is not healing; that is a benefit of sonship. His message is not deliverance; that is a privilege of sonship. His message is not holiness; that is a result of sonship. His message is centered in His desire to have sons. What does a father want? He wants sons. Well, God the Father wants sons. He has manifested what He wants in Christ. When many people look at Christ they see a Savior, they see a deliverer, a healer, a blesser of men, a soon-coming King, the lion of Judah, a conqueror, all these things. But when the Father looks at Christ, He sees **His Son**, the apple of His eye, the image of His creation, the end result of His plan. He sees what He wants, and He says, "I am well pleased."

The apostle Paul teaches that when we're born again, God places us in His Son. Not only that, he teaches that God has a predestined plan for those who are in the Son, that they be conformed to His image, "that he might be the firstborn among many brethren" (Romans 8:29). So the whole purpose of God revolves around Christ, because He is the Son. We are placed in Christ because He is the Son God wants us to be.

The message of Christ is sonship. But what is sonship? Sonship is living the life of Jesus Christ on this earth twenty-four hours a day. That's what sonship is all about, the manifesting of His life. It centers around the Father. When you ask, "What is a son?" immediately I think of the Father. And sonship is what He desires.

ANTHONY: Why isn't this message of the gospel shared more often? Why do we always get something else?

LUMAN: Because of the basic nature of man. Very few people who are believers know that gospel, because most people who are saved are saved for what they can get out of it. They're saved because they don't want to go to hell. Or they're saved because they got tired of living a life of sin, or for some other reason. Therefore their gospel centers around themselves, and what God has done for them. You know, "Thank you, Lord, for saving me." And God is God to them, but He is not Father to them. He can't be Father to them until they spend time in His Word and have the very Word of the Father impregnated in them. That's what makes a son, even in the natural. Natural birth does not make a son. It produces one, but it doesn't make one. The **word** of a natural father makes a natural son.

Being born again produces a son. When you are born again you are a son. John says, "Now are we the sons of God . . . " But he goes on to say, " . . . it doth not yet appear what we shall be: but we know that, when He shall appear, we shall be like Him; for we shall see Him as He is. And every man that hath this hope in Him purifieth himself, even as He is pure" (1 John 3:2, 3). Every believer, when he is born again, is a produced son. But he is not a made son. It takes the Word of God to bring about the son who pleases the Father, a relationship and fellowship with the Father. Very few believers have that special

fellowship that John talks about when he says, "That which we
have seen and heard declare we unto you, that ye also may have
fellowship with us: and truly our fellowship is with the
Father, and with his Son Jesus Christ" (1 John 1:3).

Now, why do most preachers preach? They will tell you
they preach to get sinners saved, or they preach for this or they
preach for that. And the Lord knows that these days many have
quit preaching even to get sinners saved. I don't know why they
preach. But anyway, what they preach is not what John said. He
didn't say, "These things declare we unto you that you might
get saved," though we know that salvation is for whosoever
will. But he said, he declared these things "that ye also may
have fellowship with us: and truly our fellowship is with the
Father, and with his Son Jesus Christ" (1 John 1:3). The apostle
Paul says, " . . . that I should preach . . . the unsearchable
riches of Christ: And to make all men see what is the fellowship
of the mystery . . . " (Ephesians 3:8, 9).

ANTHONY: It is a mystery, isn't it?

LUMAN: Yes, but what he was trying to make known was
not the mystery, but the **fellowship**. Sonship is a fellowship
with the Father, that's what it's all about. It is sharing the
fellowship that the Father and the Son have. We are brought
into it at salvation. The Holy Spirit awakens us to it and the
Word of God nourishes it.

ANTHONY: We enter into the fellowship the Father and
the Son have established. In John 17 Jesus expressed in His
prayer very explicitly, "That they all may be one; as thou,
Father, art in me, and I in thee, that they also may be one in us:
that the world may believe that thou has sent me" (John 17:21).

LUMAN: We often talk about testifying or sharing; sharing is a reality to me. But what do we share? There is a lot of
misunderstanding about that. You've been talking about fellowship. Fellowship is the part we share. You see, the Father
shares it with the Son and the Son shares it with the Father. It's a
spiritual thing, so the Holy Spirit is involved in this; He is the

medium by which it is done. So when we come into the family. You're never part of a family until you share the fellowship of it. You know, you've gone to meetings where you just sit back and watch everybody laugh and have a big time, and you feel like a left foot because you're not sharing in it. So what we share with members of the same faith is fellowship, or at least, that's what we're supposed to share. I've had people tell me, "We shared Christ." That is not so, because you don't share Christ in words. What we're doing right now, in fact is not sharing Christ; we're sharing fellowship.

Recently someone told me, "You're not sharing Christ." And for about three days I felt I had lost God. I thought, "Dear God, with all the problems we're having, and all this time I was only doing this because I thought I was sharing Christ. I thought that was what I was doing, Lord."

I examined myself, because the source of the comment was very close to me. I thought, "Lord, could it be? If that is right, then they can take all this mess I'm putting up with and stick it in their ear! I'll get out of this right now, because I don't have to take this stuff." But the Lord got me out in the middle of the country and began to deal with me. And we **are** sharing Christ. But "sharing Christ" is not in the Word. That person said that because we don't sit around and talk about Jesus all the time and have Scripture searches. That is fine, and maybe we should do more of it, but the point is, when did God share Christ?

ANTHONY: When He gave Him.

LUMAN: He was shared when He emptied out His life on the cross. Sharing Christ is the giving of a life; it's not sitting around talking. I don't care if you are talking about Jesus. Sharing Christ means giving your life twenty-four hours a day. When I saw that, I realized that many times I had been guilty of making people think my sharing Christ is me teaching a lesson to them. That's sharing fellowship with them. But sharing Christ is when I get down into the blood and sweat of just giving my life faithfully twenty-four hours a day, many times in little, mundane things, for the sake of the gospel. That is sharing Christ.

ANTHONY: There's a statement which simply says, "When I cease to bleed, I cease to bless." The Scripture says, "My little children, let us not love in word, neither in tongue; but in deed and in truth" (1 John 3:18).

James talks about the same thing when he talks about being a doer of the Word, not just a hearer. But people misunderstand that because they think they're going to go out and do something for God. How do you "do something for God?"

Doing is giving our lives. And that can only be done through the power of the Spirit.

LUMAN: There is a fine line there. People will misunderstand what I said earlier and say, "Now you're saying it's all works." That isn't it either. There's a difference between "works" and a given life.

ANTHONY: I was trying to explain this mystery to someone recently, and she made a very apt comment. She said, "Well, if Christ is Truth as you say—if Christ is everything you are talking about—then why are you here? Why don't you just go away and die somewhere. You would be happier." And this is essentially the same thing Paul was saying when he said he was "willing rather to be absent from the body, and to be present with the Lord" (2 Corinthians 5:8). The only reason we're here is for sharing. But sharing what?

I can specifically identify the date and time and location when I knew there was a spiritual rebirth in my life. But several months before that I had intellectually accepted Christ. In those intervening months I was doing all kinds of things for God. I was going to make a great witness and get elected governor and do all kinds of stuff for the Lord. I was going to get Christians elected and save the country. And then it hit me like a ton of bricks: there is nothing I can do for the Lord! That was a very sobering experience, and that is very real to a lot of people. What would you say about that, JW?

LUMAN: Praise God! Now "sharing" is not a bad word. It comes to me that what we're asking is, "What is the difference between giving your life and doing something?"

ANTHONY: There's nothing you can do in the flesh to please God.

LUMAN: Right, but here is the thing: in the family we share fellowship. I don't share the life of Christ with the Father. I share fellowship. He has shared His life with me. In the family we feed on the fellowship of the life, the mystery. This is what exhorts us in the Lord. Then with whom do we share Christ? Those outside the family.

Now, what is the sharing of Christ? Is it in words? No, not really. We declare and we proclaim. We do that because that's part of it. But basically, the sharing of Christ is the giving of a life. Jesus says it in John 12:24: "Except a grain of wheat fall into the ground and die, it abideth alone: but if it die, it bringeth forth much fruit." So the sharing of His life is the giving of our own. What is the difference between giving one's life and working? Well, really I suppose motivation is the whole thing.

If you had two people you were watching, trying to determine who is giving their life and who is not, motivation would be the only answer. You cannot judge who is and who is not giving his life.

ANTHONY: It's none of our business.

LUMAN: That's right. But it is something else to talk about it for our own clarification. And it is a thing of motivation. Only that believer knows why he is doing what he is doing, he and God. And if he is doing that for any reason other than just the pure pleasure of the Father, then he isn't giving his life. If he has selfish motives, or if it's just a job to him, he isn't giving his life. A given life is a lost life. Jesus says if you lose your life you shall keep it; if you save your life, you shall lose it. So it is actually a loss of one's life. Paul says, "I am crucified with Christ; nevertheless I live; yet not I, but Christ liveth in me: and the life which I now live in the flesh (he means twenty-four hours a day) I live by the faith (by the knowledge, by the motivation) of the Son of God . . . " (Galatians 2:20). So a given life is a life that is completely motivated by Christ.

ANTHONY: In 1 John in the Amplified version it says, "All who keep His commandments (who obey His orders, and follow His plan, live and continue to live, to stay and) abide in Him, and He in them. They let Christ be a home to them and they are the home of Christ. And by this we know and understand and have the proof that he (really) lives and makes His home in us, by the (Holy) Spirit Whom He has given us."

The interesting thing that happens in Christ is that your life from then on becomes a walk by faith. Anything you can see is no longer faith. It has to be total trust, total reliance, total dependence on Christ. You don't believe in Christ like you believe in gravity; you believe, you rely, you trust, you totally depend on. You have no life other than His. It's a new birth and a new life.

When you enter into this new life, when spiritual rebirth happens, when you know you're born to live instead of born to die, it is going to cost you something. It is going to cost you your life. And that isn't always shared. Someone listening right now might say, "Christ, so what? We've got a lot of great men. We've got Jesus Christ, and Mohammed, and Buddha, and there were all these guys. They all contributed something." This is a popular humanistic approach to the gospel. What would you say to them?

LUMAN: The whole point is this: it is not the greatness the man Jesus; the greatness is the gift of God. Mohammed, by his own confession, was not the gift of God. Buddha was not the gift of God. And neither of these men offered themselves as the very life and gift of God. Christ did. The difference is that Christ is the **very life of God** offered. To accept Christ is to accept the life that God Himself has offered. It is not the measurement of the greatness of a three and one-half year ministry, or the good things He did, or the benevolent acts He committed, or even the precepts He taught. All other religions seek to make men better. The Truth does not seek to make men better, but rather to give man, who has no life, eternal life. There is a difference. I don't need to be made better; I need life. I am dead without life.

EPILOGUE

We pray for PATIENCE: God sends tribulation
(Romans 5:3-5)

We pray for SUBMISSION: God sends suffering
(Hebrews 5:8)

We pray for UNSELFISHNESS: God asks that we sacrifice
ourselves (1 John 3:16)

We pray for VICTORY: God allows us to be
tempted (1 John 5:4)

We pray for HUMILITY: God allows messengers of
Satan to buffet us
(2 Corinthians 12:7)

We pray for STRENGTH: God reveals our secret
fears and innermost
weakness
(2 Corinthians 12:9)

We pray for UNION WITH JESUS: God severs all natural ties
and we walk alone and our
friends misunderstand
(2 Timothy 4:16)

We pray for LOVE: God sends us peculiar
suffering by sending us
unlovely people
(1 Corinthians 13:4-8)

We pray for LIKENESS TO JESUS: God puts us in the furnace
of affliction
(Matthew 20:223

MUCH THAT PERPLEXES US IS BUT AN ANSWER TO OUR PRAYERS!